Innovation, Research and Development and Capital Evaluation

Edited by Luigi Aldieri

Published in London, United Kingdom

Innovation, Research and Development and Capital Evaluation
http://dx.doi.org/10.5772/intechopen.98055
Edited by Luigi Aldieri

Contributors
Rizwan Ullah Khan, Munir A. Abbasi, Azlan Amran, Arshad Fawad, Petri P. Kärenlampi, Martin Ndzana, Gregory Mvogo, Mitali Gupta, Waldemar Milewicz, Alina Ianioglo, Elleuch Fadoi

First published in London, United Kingdom, 2022 by IntechOpen
IntechOpen is the global imprint of INTECHOPEN LIMITED, registered in England and Wales, registration number: 11086078, 5 Princes Gate Court, London, SW7 2QJ, United Kingdom

British Library Cataloguing-in-Publication Data
A catalogue record for this book is available from the British Library

Additional hard and PDF copies can be obtained from orders@intechopen.com

Innovation, Research and Development and Capital Evaluation
Edited by Luigi Aldieri
p. cm.
Print ISBN 978-1-80355-504-1
Online ISBN 978-1-80355-505-8
eBook (PDF) ISBN 978-1-80355-506-5

For EU product safety concerns:
IN TECH d.o.o., Prolaz Marije Krucifikse Kozulić 3, 51000 Rijeka, Croatia,
info@intechopen.com or visit our website at intechopen.com.

Meet the editor

Luigi Aldieri is a Full Professor of Economics at the Department of Economic and Statistical Sciences of the University of Salerno. He holds a Ph.D. in Sciences Economiques et de gestion at the Solvay Business School of Economics and Management (SBS-EM) of Université Libre de Bruxelles (ULB). His Ph.D. thesis "Three Essays on Knowledge Diffusion and Firms' Economic Performance" is supervised by Prof. Michele Cincera. His research interests embrace Applied Econometrics, the measurement of knowledge, geographic spillovers, and economic performance of large international firms, as well as the empirical analysis of the effects of educational level on fertility in developed countries.

Contents

Preface

The text investigates the interactions among innovation, entrepreneurship, and ecosystems.

Chapter 1 investigates family firm entrepreneurial strategies' impact on innovation ability during new venture step and reveals how family firms take an initial step for the outcome. Basically, family firms are often assumed to be conservative in their innovation strategy. However, the truth is that many family-owned businesses are amongst the most innovative in their industries. Moreover, many of them can thrive across generations, which indicates that the spirit of innovation is at the very heart of their company culture. In addition, to adjust according to market demand and uncertainty, top management or founder must modify the in-hand resources according to the market demand. Nevertheless, due to the current era of digital globalization due to Covid 19, family-owned small and medium-sized enterprises face many challenges to sustain for the long term in the uncertain market. Therefore, strategic policymakers are needed to replace or modify the current business model by adopting digital technologies. Because without adoption of digital entrepreneurial activities cannot sustain for the long term. Therefore, the current study gives several suggestions to the policymakers and governmental institutions to replace and modify the existing resources and capabilities through digital technologies.

Chapter 2 investigates the relationship between formality and SME innovation. Specifically, the analysis considers the impact of formality on product, process, organizational, and commercial innovation. The research methodology is based on the analysis of the IRDC data set from Cameroon and Senegal. The authors use a logit model. The results show that formality significantly determines the capacity of firm innovation. Besides, the role of formality varies depending on the type of innovation, the sector of activity, and the country. It is therefore essential to intensify initiatives aimed at the formalization of businesses to improve SME innovation in French-speaking Africa and move from simple copying of innovations and their adaptation to real innovations that can impact growth. On this issue, Cameroonian public authorities are even more concerned because not only does the rate of informality remain very high in Cameroon, but the impact of formality remains insignificant, especially when considering the frequency of innovation.

Chapter 3 will explore the impact of a foreign investor on the development of Bank Pekao S.A. A literature review will be applied for this aim. It covers a detailed analysis of transaction documentation and post-audit statements of both the Supreme Audit Office as well as delegations of the Ministry of State Treasury. Thanks to research it can be assessed how UniCredito Italiano has positively influenced the operation of Pekao S.A. after the acquisition of shares. Thereby, the results of this study contest popular opinion about the exploitation of domestic employees by foreign companies.

From the methodological point of view, there are many definitions of foreign direct investment. The subject of this article leads to a special emphasis on definitions which refer to the creation of a long-term relationship between an investor and the company in which the shares are acquired.

In line with the special attention paid to ecosystem conditions that encourage innovation and entrepreneurship, Chapter 4 provides a critical review and expands the understanding of the concepts of the innovation ecosystem and entrepreneurial ecosystem. The entrepreneurial ecosystem represents a collection of actors that interact within a geographically bound entrepreneurial environment and factors, which contribute to the development of productive entrepreneurship. Innovation ecosystems represent communities of interacting actors that support innovation processes and create technologies and innovations. The focus of the innovation ecosystem is on value creation through the creation of innovations, while the focus of the entrepreneurship ecosystem is on the development of entrepreneurship. There are differences between the two concepts, but also the relationships and interactions, which are revealed in the chapter. Also, there are highlighted the framework, components and features of both entrepreneurial and innovation ecosystems.

Chapter 5 discusses the important role of capital evaluation. In particular, the capital return rate is the relative time change rate of value. Correspondingly, the current value can be produced in terms of value change rate divided by capital return rate. There is a variety of ways to approximate the expected capital return rate. These are briefly discussed. The approximation of the value change rate is still more variant, depending on the type of businesses discussed. A variety of businesses may appear within a firm, in which case the value change rates must be integrated. An example is provided of a real estate firm benefiting from the growth of multiannual plants of varying ages. It is found that the application of a duration-dependent reference capital return rate increases the value increment rate of juvenile stands and decreases that of mature stands, however increasing the valuation result of both.

Chapter 6 considers a centralized one-echelon supply chain with two retailers selling products and facing stochastic demand. Given the large distance between the supplier and retailers, and the corresponding large fixed transportation cost (by order) long replenishment cycles are typically used. In such situations, transporting stocks between retailers is much easier and less costly, and may be done on a more frequent basis. In this work, the authors explore the cost benefits of allowing multiple shipments between retailers during a supplier replenishment cycle. Items' transshipment between retailers still involves of course certain costs, for handling and moving the items. Since multiple items can often be shipped on a single pallet, part of those costs will be independent of the number of items shipped. Instead of only including a variable transport cost per item, the authors also include a fixed transport cost per shipment.

Finally, Chapter 7 attempts to understand New Product Development Approaches and Strategies adopted by key global and domestic brands operating in the Indian Textile market and derive lessons for the development of future models of New Product Development in the Indian Textile and Apparel Industry. The brands have been selected on the basis of their popularity and position in the Indian Textile markets. Indian players: The Raymond Group and Siyaram's particularly cater to the men's clothing range only. With the advent of the multinational brands like Allen Solly into the Indian markets, women's formal as well as comfortable casual clothing range has been given due attention over the period of time. It may also seem that women's apparel garments only came into being after the substantial rise in their numbers in the workplace otherwise there might be a connotation in the minds of the companies that formal wear is only about men's clothing and perhaps the monopoly of it. Secondly, Casual/Comfort wear clothing is the largest category in terms of market size and a lot of small and large players have come up which though not mentioned in the current paper but constitute a substantial market size in the Indian Readymade Garments Industry. Thus there is a lot of scope for New Product Development in this category of clothing segment which so far has not been done by the Indian brands which have largely followed the trends and patterns of international brands. Thirdly, the discussions in this chapter have confirmed the hypothesis that the most sought-after strategies of New Product Development have been launching of the New Product Lines followed by the Additions to the Product Lines/Product Improvement. New-to-the-World Products have been particularly pursued by multinational brands like Van Heusen. Apart from this, it is also to be realised by the apparel brands that apart from the elite section, India has a large middle-income segment that can be cashed on to the fullest potential. But so far the brands only have capitalised on the premium and elite class. Thus, there is a need for the Indian brands to catch up with the multinational brands so as to become more competitive in the domestic and overseas markets which would only be possible by developing an extensive innovation culture and capabilities of the small innovative firms on the part of the policy-making institutions in India.

Luigi Aldieri
Department of Economic and Statistical Sciences,
University of Salerno,
Fisciano, Italy

Chapter 1

The Innovative Business Model for Family-Owned Firms in the Era of Digital Entrepreneurship: Evidence from Emerging Economy

Rizwan Ullah Khan, Munir A. Abbasi, Azlan Amran and Arshad Fawad

Abstract

The current Covid-19 pandemic has been changed the businesses plans. High uncertainty can compel the organization to change the business plan according to the market demand. In the current era of digitalization, organizations are needed to modify the existing business plan and innovate it through technologies. Modifying existing resources according to the market demand is challenging for the organization; employers face many challenges and obstacles. Businesses plan to develop a long-term business model to validate the attractiveness, reduce the avoidable investment of scarce resources, and structure the business process. In the current era of digitalization, businesses, specifically, SMEs cannot compete with the competitors who can adopt digitalization systems. Therefore, the current chapter is trying to find out the challenges faced by SMEs in developing economies during the adoption of the digital business model. In the current chapter, researchers focus on three different kinds of digital technologies that must be part of the business model during the era of digitalization, such as adopting digital technologies (artificial intelligence, Internet of Thing, and virtual reality and to create a new business model following the current era issue, these are the main block to resist of these market uncertainties in a new venture of family firms.

Keywords: digitalization, entrepreneurship, business model innovation, artificial intelligence (AI), internet of things (IoT), virtual reality (VR), Pakistan

1. Introduction

This chapter investigates family firm entrepreneurial strategies' impact on innovation ability during new venture step and reveals how family firms take an initial step for the outcome. Basically, family firms are often assumed to be conservative in their innovation strategy. However, the truth is that many family-owned businesses are among the most innovative in their industries. Moreover, many of them can thrive across generations, which indicates that the spirit of innovation is at the very heart of their company culture.

In addition, to adjust according to market demand and uncertainty, top management or founder must modify the in-hand resources according to the market demand.

Nowadays, the era of digital entrepreneurship, such as new technology, machine learning, and artificial intelligence (AI) due to the COVID-19 pandemic, has changed how companies of all sectors and regions do business [1]. Due to digital entrepreneurship has transformed 50% of daily business activities from physical to virtual form [2], as a result, many firms have banked corruption, which negatively impacts unemployment and economic growth. In addition, Nicola et al. [3] suggested that more than 30% of small firms have been stopped their activities in developed, while 60% in developing economies [4]. Therefore, to stay competitive advantage during this pandemic, this business and economic development must adopt new strategies and practices [5]. Therefore, the firm's policymakers started to modify the current business model as per the digital entrepreneurial era; the firm's business model can be understood as a core of a firm to create and deliver values for its customers and to capture value for itself [6]. A business model is a holistic perception and planning of the firm on the overall tenure and process. There are two models, the cost model and the revenue model. Consequently, COVID-19 pandemic shifts the whole business activities through online sources, because entrepreneurial digitalization has negatively affected small- and medium-sized enterprises (SMEs) [7], because small ventures or founder stage SMEs deploy lack of resources and capabilities [8, 9].

Additionally, small- and medium-sized enterprises are an essential factor for economic growth and the primary source of employment creation. In the globe, more than 80% are SMEs, contributing to 55% in developed economies and 35% in developing economies, with a 65 to 80% employment ratio [10]. In small enterprises, 95% of enterprises are owned and controlled by family members [11]. As stated, family firms are the most dominant form of business organization globally, and the impact of these firms on economies worldwide is notable [12]. For example, in Germany, more than 90% of all companies are family-controlled, and nearly 90% are family-managed. The latter generate 48% of overall turnover and employ nearly 60% of all insurance-liable employees, a number that continued to grow as the number of jobs expanded by more than 11% from 2006 to 2012 [13].

Therefore, this chapter tries to shed light on the family firm's ability to modify the previous business model according to digital entrepreneurship. This chapter specifically highlighted the family firms because family firms have idiosyncrasies and non-economic characteristics [14], differentiating them from non-family firms. In the founder stage, family firms are more risk-averse and concentrate on sustaining long-term ownership [15]. Therefore, family firms face a considerable challenge during the digital globalization era to adopt a business model and answer customer demands.

1.1 Definition of family firms

Defining family firms have become a considerable contradiction among the researchers because defining family firms vary from industry to industry and country to country. There is no specific definition to explain the features and characteristics of family firms.

Nowadays, academicians and practitioners focus entirely on family firms because family firms have different strategic decisions and features compared to non-family firms. In addition, the family firm's final objective is different from the non-family firms (e.g., risk-aversion, non-financial, lack of confidence, etc.). Furthermore, family firms offer idiosyncratic characteristics (e.g., family ownership, family member involvement in decision-making) and motivation (a transgenerational success that substantially affects the firm's strategic behaviors) [16]. In addition, to define family firms, this question does not necessarily have an immediate and defensive answer. Instead, there are many ways to define family firms; the main differentiated factor of family firms from non-family firms can divide through three methodologies: 1) firm ownership, 2) firm governance, and 3) a combination of firm ownership and governance. Nevertheless, the most common approach of defining family firms is the largest ownership share and governance.

As abovementioned, family firms can be differentiated based on two main idiosyncratic characteristics (e.g., ownership and family members in top management) from non-family firms, these two characteristics can vary on from each sector to sector and country to country, see to **Table 1**, and each country has been defining family firms based on their proportion between ownership and family members in top management. Furthermore, Stanley et al. [23] suggested that in developed economies, the involvement of family members in top management is preferred as compared to ownership, because Clinton et al.'s [24] finding reveals that family firms can sustain their generational transformation up to fourth and fifth generation very smoothly; in addition, they have a very strong family business background and risk-averse as compared to emerging economies [25].

Accordingly, this chapter will be following the combination of a family member's share in ownership and involvement in top management as to the previous studies, because it will be conducted in Pakistan. In the Pakistani context, family firms will be defined as those SMEs that have less than 250 employees [26–28] and also have more than 50% family-owned and controlled by family members (at least in the second generation) and in which the business family is involved in top management [29, 30].

Country	Criteria	Definition	Author(s)
Portugal	Ownership, family involvement, succession	In Portugal a firm is called family-owned when the family members are involved in the ownership and take part in the decision making.	[17]
United States	Ownership, family involvement, management	Family firms are those where at least two family members employed in the firms	[18]
United Kingdom	Culture	The family firm is defined in the UK, which are following the culture transcends and is completed, and it is the combination of family-owned attributes and firms itself.	[19]
China	Family involvement, management	At least one family member on the management team.	National Bureau of Statistics of China (2009) (http://www.stats.gov.cn/english/)
Italy	Family involvement, management	where a family owns at least 50% of the shares and at least one family member is involved in management.	[20]
Malaysia	Ownership and management	51% or more of the firm's owners had to be in the hands of a family member and family members	[21]
India	Controlling system and management	"any form of business association where the voting control is in the hands of a given family"	[22]

Source: Author self-created.

Table 1.
Definition of family-owned SMEs in different context.

2. Digital technologies supporting business models

Digital technologies such as AI, VR, and IoT are affecting people living style and working environment, and generating new thoughts for solving of the problem or surviving their lives, and increase the fascination of individuals, the public, and societies [31]. In the era of digitalization, digital technologies are very supportive in case of reducing cost iteration and experimentation of new ideas creates the possibilities of adopting new ideas and concepts [32].

2.1 Artificial intelligence

Artificial intelligence is one more fascinating technology in the era of digitalization. For a definition, we support Copeland [33], to define artificial intelligence as "the ability of the digital computer to perform task commonly associated intelligent beings." Moreover, Copeland expands the approach of artificial intelligence by the components that make up intelligence, such as problem solving, language, perception, learning, and reasoning. Additionally, AI helps the businesses to adopt such new technologies because it supports in case of understanding customer demands. Therefore, in the current era, the adoption of AI is very important and the modification of existing business plans with new long-term objectives.

2.2 Virtual reality

Construct such as virtual reality (VR) and artificial intelligence mostly similar and interchangeable, which makes a barrier between mangers, and entrepreneurs to explore their potential and effectiveness. VR represents the digitalization of the actual things in the digital contents and information, VR is basically the replacement of the actual things to the virtual. The best example of the VR is three-dimensional (3D) digital environment created by computers. Hence, in the era of digitalization, the organization can modify their business plan toward digital entrepreneurship that innovates something digitally which is different from the competitor [34].

2.3 Internet of things

Internet of things is the best source of opportunity recognition, due to digitalization, and organizations is needed to innovate new things to fulfill the customer's needs. In that era, if an organization adopted the IoT, it can easily innovate the new products and services through low cost and less time wasting [35]. Hence, it is the best technology, if any organization has the ability to adapt in an uncertain situation, can easily compete in the market.

3. Initiative steps of family-owned entrepreneurs toward digitalization

As abovementioned that family firms are the dominant platform of a business in the globe, additionally, Randolph et al. [36] suggested that family firms are the main contributor to economic growth and employment creation. Furthermore, Stanley et al. [23] scrutinized that family firms are more initiative and accept the new challenge as compared to non-family firms. Instead of the significant contribution of family firms toward economic growth and employment creation, in the current era of digitalization due to the COVID-19 pandemic, the family firms are facing a lot of challenges and barriers to sustaining their position in the market. The reasons behind the high failure rate of family firms are family firms having family members in their top management and in strategic decision making, those having a lack of resources and capabilities to defend the external market fluctuation [8]. Consequently, the family members are needed to adopt the digital entrepreneurial capabilities and for replace and be aided by technology-driven innovation, such as artificial intelligence (AI), internet of things (IoT), and virtual reality (VR). Digitalization refers to the digital conversation of information and knowledge, and it also concerned with a comprehensive implication of such processes and their effect on the socioeconomic system [37].

Additionally, top management of family firms is needed to adopt or replace the existing resources and capabilities according to the external market of digitalization, because resources and capabilities will support the mechanisms through which family firm's top management influences digital entrepreneurship or (business model innovation) [38], and the previous studies postulate that to sustain family firms in the era of digitalization might require an adapted set of resources and capabilities [39, 40], existing resources such as sales, marketing, human resources, operation, finance, research and development, and customer need to transform into digital environment [41]. Moreover, the external market fluctuation can compel the top management to modify the existing business model and adopt new digital technologies according to the market demand. First and almost, the firm needed to modify the ongoing strategies according to the era, because management transformation is the first step to create an innovative idea and design thinking [42].

Furthermore, family business strategic thinking is different from the non-family firms, because family firms during the founder stage are planning to sustain the firm survival and family ownership for long term [43]. Hence, the policymakers are needed to modify the in-hand resources according to the current era of digital entrepreneurship. In addition, digital transformation motivates the top management regarding innovation and creative design planning [44]. Therefore, this chapter trying to discriminate the initiative steps of family firms toward the digital entrepreneurship. Henceforward, we have created a Mosley's hierarchy model of business for family firms in the era of digital entrepreneurial (see **Figure 1**). The figure represents that first and almost, top management is needed to think about that how to modify the existing resources and capabilities. Next, to modify or replace the existing resources and capabilities can encourage toward new ideas through innovative way and following the current demand of the market. Third, combining the creative ideas and core resources and capabilities is trying to construct or operate the product/services. Last step, top management can utilize the digital resources and capabilities according to the new initiative way. So, these four steps are repeated for developing the new product that is called business model innovation (BMI) *according to the era of digitalization (see* **Figure 2** *for more details).*

4. Family firm cycle of digital business model innovation

The current era of digitalization has affected of all kinds of firms and industries [46, 47], it is defined as that techniques, process, tools, and methods depend on a series of binary digits [48] such as cloud computing and data analysis [49]. Moreover, previous studies postulate that the adoption of digital technologies is the

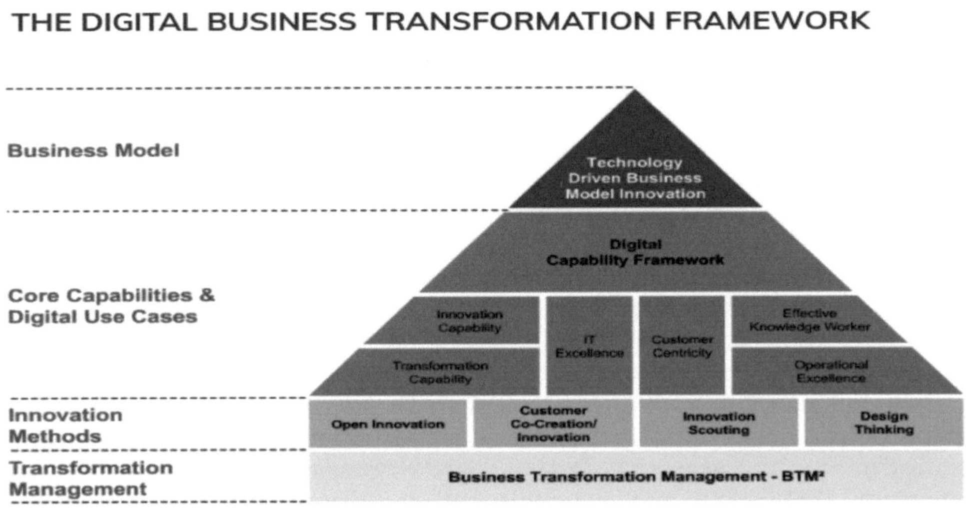

Figure 1.
Business model in case of Mosley Hierarchy.

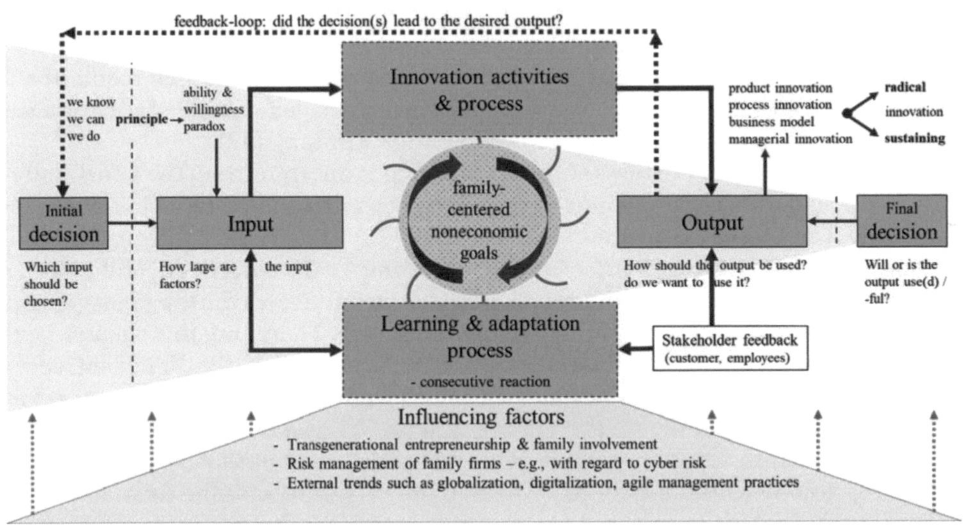

Figure 2.
Feninger et al.'s [45] family firms' innovation as a circular process.

main contributor for a long-term survival of a firm [50, 51] and also plays a pivotal role to sustain the competitive advantage [52, 53]. Additionally, top management of family firms is needed to enhance the entrepreneurial ability of digital technologies and commercialize them, and to do that, the firm requires a proper business model [54].

More precisely, to survive with the external market fluctuation tempted by digital technologies, firms are needed to follow the digital business innovation [40, 55], which is in accordance with Fichman et al. [56], explaining that for a significant and creative way of capturing business values that is embodied in or enabling digital technologies the main contributor of the generated business value.

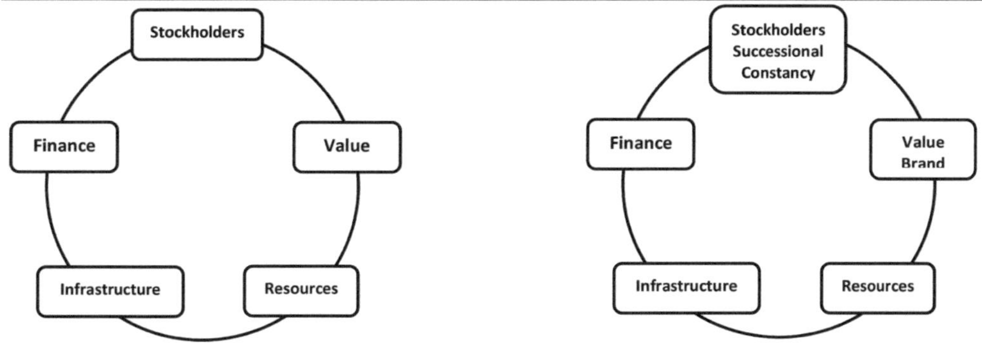

Table 2.
Family firms are planning different business model.

Additionally, family firms are planning different business models as compared to non-family firms (see to **Table 2** for more details), during the start-up have different final objectives, and during the founder stage, family firms are mostly focused on the family members' control and survival for long term. Furthermore, the family firm's top management is very high risk averse as compared to the second and third generations because in the start-up founder invest their saving and all bank balance to start a business. Consequently, during the founder stage, top management cannot bold decision for any investment [57]. Besides all these idiosyncrasies characteristics could be replace or modify due to external market uncertainty.

As abovementioned, the family firm's top management can gain confidence from generation to generation, as we discussed before family firms is taking more confidential decisions as compared to the founder stage [58].

5. Conclusion

This chapter tried to explore the digital technologies (internet of things, artificial intelligence, and virtual reality), impact of family-owned firms, business model innovation in the era of digitalization. Hence, due to the current COVID-19 pandemic, each organization is shifting from reality toward the virtual. Therefore, the top management realizes adopting a digital business model to fulfill the customer requirement and sustain competitive advantage. The researcher focuses on the three leading digital technologies and chooses these technologies based on interviews. Before starting the study, the researcher interviewed the top management of the manufacturing firms of Pakistan. In an interview, the researcher asked the top management regarding the main issue or challenges about technologies, so more than 80 percent of employers tick these technologies and show remarks that in the era of digitalization; these three technologies are the core solution fulfilling the customer's: needs.

Hence, this study's finding reveals that employers and entrepreneurs are suggested to focus on these digital technologies and modify the existing business plan according to the market demands. So, these technologies can help the business innovate new things at low cost, get information, and design different products through virtual reality technology; these are the best source of competitive advantage in the era of digitalization. Additionally, government agencies and institutions are needed to support the business in adopting new technologies that create such an environment facility through information and awareness.

Family firms are chosen because they are the more dominant form of business globally [59]; family firms are the main contributor toward economic growth and employment creation. There are more than 90% of firms are owned and controlled by family members. Despite their significant contribution to the economy and employment, family firms are very risk-averse compared to non-family firms, and their existence is fundamental.

Nevertheless, due to the current era of digital globalization due to COVID-19, family-owned small- and medium-sized enterprises face many challenges to sustain for the long term in the uncertain market. Therefore, strategic policymakers are needed to replace or modify the current business model through adopting digital technologies. Because without adoption of digital entrepreneurial activities cannot sustain for long term. Therefore, this study gives several suggestions to the policymakers and governmental institutions to replace and modify the existing resources and capabilities through digital technologies.

Author details

Rizwan Ullah Khan[1*], Munir A. Abbasi[2], Azlan Amran[1] and Arshad Fawad[3]

1 Graduate School of Business, Universiti Sains Malaysia, Pulao Penang, Malaysia

2 Benazir School of Business, Benazir Bhutto Shaheed University, Karachi, Pakistan

3 School of Economics and Management, Southwest Jiaotong University, China

*Address all correspondence to: rizwanhayat1989@gmail.com

References

[1] Soltanifar M, Hughes M, Göcke L. Digital Entrepreneurship: Impact on Business and Society. Cham, Switzerland: Springer Nature; 2021. p. 327

[2] Bican PM, Brem A. Digital business model, digital transformation, digital entrepreneurship: Is there a sustainable "digital"? Sustainability. 2020;**12**(13):5239

[3] Nicola M, Alsafi Z, Sohrabi C, Kerwan A, Al-Jabir A, Iosifidis C, et al. The socio-economic implications of the coronavirus and COVID-19 pandemic: A review. International Journal of Surgery. 2020;**78**(2020):185-193

[4] Anyanwu MU, Festus IJ, Nwobi OC, Jaja CJI, Oguttu JW. A perspective on Nigeria's preparedness, response and challenges to mitigating the spread of COVID-19. Challenges. 2020;**11**(2):22

[5] Akpan IJ, Soopramanien D, Kwak DH. Cutting-edge technologies for small business and innovation in the era of COVID-19 global health pandemic. Journal of Small Business & Entrepreneurship. 2020:1-11

[6] Göck L. Business Model Development in the Field of Tension between Multinational Companies. Wiesbaden, Germany: Springer Fachmedien Wiesbaden; 2016

[7] Eduardsen J. Internationalisation through digitalisation: The impact of E-commerce usage on internationalisation in small-and medium-sized firms. In: International Business in the Information and Digital Age. UK: Emerald Publishing Limited; 2018

[8] Khan RU, Salamzadeh Y, Kawamorita H, Rethi G. Entrepreneurial orientation and small and medium-sized enterprises performance; Does 'access to finance' moderate the relation in emerging economies? Vision. 2021;**25**(1):88-102

[9] Khan RU, Arif H, Sahar NE, Ali A, Abbasi MA. The role of financial resources in SMEs financial and environmental performance; The mediating role of green innovation. Green Finance. 2022a;**4**(1):36-53

[10] Ndiaye N, Razak LA, Nagayev R, Ng A. Demystifying small and medium enterprises (SMEs) performance in emerging and developing economies. Borsa Istanbul Review. 2018;**18**(4):269-281

[11] Oudah M, Jabeen F, Dixon C. Determinants linked to family business sustainability in the UAE: An AHP approach. Sustainability. 2018;**10**(1):246

[12] De Massis A, Frattini F, Majocchi A, Piscitello L. Family firms in the global economy: Toward a deeper understanding of internationalization determinants, processes, and outcomes. Global Strategy Journal. 2018;**8**(1):3-21

[13] Cravotta S, Grottke M. Digitalization in German family firms–some preliminary insights. Journal of Evolutionary Studies in Business. 2019;**4**(1):1-25

[14] Randolph RV, Alexander BN, Debicki BJ, Zajkowski R. Untangling non-economic objectives in family & non-family SMEs: A goal systems approach. Journal of Business Research. 2019;**98**:317-327

[15] Lumpkin GT, Brigham KH. Long–term orientation and intertemporal choice

in family firms. Entrepreneurship Theory and Practice. 2011;**35**(6):1149-1169

[16] Brumana M, Minola T, Garrett RP, Digan SP. How do family firms launch new businesses? A developmental perspective on internal corporate venturing in family business. Journal of Small Business Management. 2017;**55**(4):594-613

[17] Gallo MÁ, Tàpies J, Cappuyns K. Comparison of family and nonfamily business: Financial logic and personal preferences. Family Business Review. 2004;**17**(4):303-318

[18] Martínez AB, Galván RS, Palacios TMB. An empirical study about knowledge transfer, entrepreneurial orientation and performance in family firms. European Journal of International Management. 2016;**10**(5):534-557

[19] Ramos HM, Man TWY, Mustafa M, Ng ZZ. Psychological ownership in small family firms: Family and non-family employees work attitudes and behaviours. Journal of Family Business Strategy. 2014;**5**(3):300-311

[20] Cascino S, Pugliese A, Mussolino D, Sansone C. The influence of family ownership on the quality of accounting information. Family Business Review. 2010;**23**(3):246-265

[21] Mustafa MJ, Elliott C. The curious case of human resource development in family-small-to-medium sized enterprises. Human Resource Development Quarterly. 2019;**30**(3):281-290

[22] Merchant P, Kumar A, Mallik D. Factors influencing family business continuity in Indian small and medium enterprises (SMEs). Journal of Family and Economic Issues. 2018;**39**(2):177-190

[23] Stanley LJ, Hernández-Linares R, López-Fernández MC, Kellermanns FW. A typology of family firms: An investigationofentrepreneurialorientation and performance. Family Business Review. 2019;**32**(2):174-194

[24] Clinton E, McAdam M, Gamble JR. Transgenerational entrepreneurial family firms: An examination of the business model construct. Journal of Business Research. 2018;**90**:269-285

[25] Zahra SA. Technological capabilities and international expansion: The moderating role of family and non-family firms social capital. Asia Pacific Journal of Management. 2019;**37**(2):1-25

[26] Alkahtani A, Nordin N, Khan RU. Does government support enhance the relation between networking structure and sustainable competitive performance among SMEs? Journal of Innovation and Entrepreneurship. 2020;**9**(1):1-16

[27] Khan RU. Relationship of HR practices and career path: A perspective of accounting studies. Jinnah Business Review. 2019;**7**(1):46-56

[28] Khan RU, Mehmood A, Ahmed M, Mustafa MJ, Alshamsi MK, Iqbal Q, et al. Impact of network structure on sustainable competitive performance among Pakistani small and medium enterprises: Does government financial support matter? Journal of Global Entrepreneurship Research. 2022b:1-13

[29] Abdullah F, Shah A, Gohar R, Iqbal AM. The effect of group and family ownership on firm performance: Empirical evidence from Pakistan. International Review of Business Research Papers. 2011;**7**(4):191-208

[30] Chang AA, Mubarik MS, Naghavi N. Passing on the legacy: Exploring the dynamics of succession in family businesses in Pakistan. Journal

of Family Business Management. 2021;**11**(2):161-184

[31] Bruno C, Canina M. Creativity 4.0. Empowering creative process for digitally enhanced people. The Design Journal. 2019;**22**(sup1):2119-2131

[32] Austin R (2016). Unleashing Creativity with Digital Technology. Available from: https://sloanreview.mit.edu/article/unleashing-creativity-with-digital-technology/

[33] Copeland BJ, (2020). Artificial Intelligence. Britannica. Available from: https://www.britannica.com/technology/artificialintelligence/Reasoning

[34] Farshid M, Paschen J, Eriksson T, Kietzmann J. Go boldly!: Explore augmented reality (AR), virtual reality (VR), and mixed reality (MR) for business. Business Horizons. 2018;**61**(5):657-663

[35] Gardner H, Weinstein E. Creativity: The view from Big C and the introduction of tiny c. In: Sternberg R, Kaufman J, editors. The Nature of Human Creativity. New York, NY: Cambridge University Press; 2018. pp. 94-109

[36] Randolph RV, Fang HC, Memili E, Nayir DZ. Family and non-family sources of knowledge diversity in family firms: The role of causation logics. International Small Business Journal. 2021;**39**(1):64-85

[37] Parviainen P, Tihinen M, Kääriäinen J, Teppola S. Tackling the digitalization challenge: How to benefit from digitalization in practice. International Journal of Information Systems and Project Management. 2017;**5**(1):63-77

[38] Duran P, Kammerlander N, Van Essen M, Zellweger T. Doing more with less: Innovation input and output in family firms. Academy of Management Journal. 2016;**59**(4):1224-1264

[39] Nambisan S. Digital entrepreneurship: Toward a digital technology perspective of entrepreneurship. Entrepreneurship Theory and Practice. 2017;**41**(6):1029-1055

[40] Teece DJ. Profiting from innovation in the digital economy: Enabling technologies, standards, and licensing models in the wireless world. Research Policy. 2018;**47**(8):1367-1387

[41] Bounfour A. Digital Futures, Digital Transformation. PI. Cham: Springer; 2016. DOI: 10.1007/978-3-319-23279-9

[42] Aslam F, Aimin W, Li M, Ur Rehman K. Innovation in the era of IoT and industry 5.0: Absolute innovation management (AIM) framework. Information. 2020;**11**(2):124

[43] Ahmad S, Omar R, Quoquab F. Family firms sustainable longevity: The role of family involvement in business and innovation capability. Journal of Family Business Management. 2020

[44] Dugstad J, Eide T, Nilsen ER, Eide H. Towards successful digital transformation through co-creation: A longitudinal study of a four-year implementation of digital monitoring technology in residential care for persons with dementia. BMC Health Services Research. 2019;**19**(1):1-17

[45] Feninger M, Kammerlander N, De Massis A. Family business innovation: A circular process model. In: Family Firms and Institutional Contexts. Edward Elgar Publishing; 2019

[46] Sorescu A. Data-driven business model innovation. Journal of Product Innovation Management. 2017;**34**(5):691-696

[47] Teece DJ. Business models and dynamic capabilities. Long Range Planning. 2018;**51**(1):40-49

[48] von Briel F, Davidsson P, Recker J. Digital technologies as external enablers of new venture creation in the IT hardware sector. Entrepreneurship Theory and Practice. 2018;**42**(1):47-69

[49] Soluk J, Miroshnychenko I, Kammerlander N, De Massis A. Family influence and digital business model innovation: The enabling role of dynamic capabilities. Entrepreneurship Theory and Practice. 2021;**45**(4):867-905

[50] Bharadwaj AS. A resource-based perspective on information technology capability and firm performance: An empirical investigation. MIS Quarterly. 2000:169-196

[51] George G, Lakhani K, Puranam P. What has changed? The impact of Covid pandemic on the technology and innovation management research agenda. Journal of Management Studies. 2020;**57**(8):1755-1758

[52] Nambisan S, Lyytinen K, Majchrzak A, Song M. Digital Innovation Management: Reinventing innovation management research in a digital world. MIS Quarterly. 2017;**41**(1)

[53] Pavlou PA, El Sawy OA. The "third hand": IT-enabled competitive advantage in turbulence through improvisational capabilities. Information Systems Research. 2010;**21**(3):443-471

[54] Chesbrough H. Business model innovation: opportunities and barriers. Long Range Planning. 2010;**43**(2-3):354-363

[55] Teece DJ. Business models, business strategy and innovation. Long Range Planning. 2010;**43**(2-3):172-194

[56] Fichman RG, Dos Santos BL, Zheng Z. Digital innovation as a fundamental and powerful concept in the information systems curriculum. MIS Quarterly. 2014;**38**(2):329-A15

[57] Martínez-García I, Basco R, Gómez-Ansón S. Dancing with giants: Contextualizing state and family ownership effects on firm performance in the Gulf Cooperation Council. Journal of Family Business Strategy. 2021:100373

[58] Arzubiaga U, Maseda A, Iturralde T. Exploratory and exploitative innovation in family businesses: The moderating role of the family firm image and family involvement in top management. Review of Managerial Science. 2019;**13**(1):1-31

[59] Berrone P, Duran P, Gómez-Mejía L, Heugens PP, Kostova T, van Essen M. Impact of informal institutions on the prevalence, strategy, and performance of family firms: A meta-analysis. Journal of International Business Studies. 2020:1-25

Chapter 2

Formality and Innovation in French-Speaking Sub-Saharan African SME: Cases of Cameroon and Senegal

Martin Ndzana and Gregory Mvogo

Abstract

Despite the importance of public policies in favor of the formalization of enterprises in French-speaking Sub-Saharan Africa, the productive fabric remains marked by a strong predominance of informal enterprises whose weight tends to limit the propensity of enterprises to innovate. In this context, becoming formal for an enterprise can improve the innovation capacity of enterprises. This article aims to analyze the role of formality on product, process, organizational and commercial innovations in Cameroon and Senegal. The results obtained using a sample of 1369 firms from data collected by the International Development Research Centre (IDRC) and logistic regression show that formal firms have a better innovation capacity. But the role of formality on innovation tends to be less important for Cameroonian firms. These results show that the Cameroonian authorities must intensify measures in favor of the formalization of enterprises to boost the potential for innovation within enterprises.

Keywords: Informality, Innovation, R&D, SMEs, Francophone Sub-Saharan Africa

1. Introduction

For several years, innovation, which has become a full-fledged field of research in economics and management, has been the subject of abundant literature. Indeed, innovation enables Small and Medium-sized Enterprises (SME) to cope, by improving their competitiveness and preserving comparative advantage [1–3] to the uncertainty of the environment caused by the globalization of economies and the constant evolution of the market for their products due to the rapid dissemination of information [4]. Thus, an innovation is defined as the introduction on the market of a new or significantly modified product or the introduction of production processes, of methods concerning the provision of services or the delivery of products, of support activity new or significantly modified or the introduction of new or significantly improved solutions concerning the organization or marketing [5] impact the performance of SME [6–8]. However, this impact depends on the level of development of the economies.

In low-income countries in general and in Francophone Sub-Saharan Africa (FSA) in particular, the productive fabric is dominated by SME, the majority of which are informal. Although there are several obstacles to the expansion of these enterprises in these economies, including the weak incentive of government policies, access to finance [9] which tend to keep them informal, they are an important source of productivity [10]. The contribution of the informal sector is predominant in the national production of these economies. For example, in Cameroon, the informal sector represents 57.6% of national production and employs nearly 90% of workers [11]. Similarly in Senegal, the informal sector contributes 51.5% to national production and employs 48.8% of the active population. A major determinant of this economic dynamic is the innovation capacity of these firms because innovation allows each of them to achieve a positive performance [7, 12]. However, if formality plays an essential role in the performance of SME [13]; it can also strongly determine their capacity to innovate. Establishing the relationship between formality and innovation is relevant.

In the literature, innovation is the subject of several studies [14–17]. That the majority of this work is concentrated in developed economies [18–21], we note an increase in developing economies [22, 23]. These essentially attest that innovation determines the performance of SME. Furthermore, that this work has addressed the issue of innovation by highlighting the comparison by activity sector and by the size of the firms, neglecting the importance of the nature of the company. Innovation having made the postulate that firm are homogeneous. However, in these economies, there are concurrently formal firms and informal, each with innovation capabilities specific to their nature [24]. Only a few studies have attempted to fill this gap. So we offer many extensions on the existing literature.

First, considering the study of [25] of firms in Kenya, the authors analyze the fact for a firm to start its activities by being casual about its capacity for innovation. However, while they attest that a firm's informal past harms its propensity to innovate, their study does not address the firm's ability to develop several innovations simultaneously. Concerning their study, we analyze not the fact of starting informal, but the fact for the SME to carry out its activities in being formal or informal on innovation. We are therefore following the work of [26] carried out in Ghana without however analyzing the consequences on performance. Our analysis, therefore, aims to be integrative by understanding the effect of innovation on industrial firms as well as on service and trade companies, since the latter is predominant in ASF. Second, not only that we explore the formality-innovation link in SME, but we also take into account that SME are not a homogenous firm size category because of different resources, capabilities and obstacles they encounter [27]. Thus, we separately analyze not only SME companies, but also large firms for the comparative purposes. Third, we propose a comparative analysis between two countries (Cameroon and Senegal) using direct measures of innovation. Although these two countries are French-speaking, they nevertheless belong to different economic zones[1], making the comparison relevant. Therefore, given the low level of integration within EMCCA, we can expect that the challenges of innovation within Cameroonian SME will be lower than in Senegal. Finally, considering that companies develop several forms of innovation

[1] Cameroon is a member country of the Economic and Monetary Community of Central Africa (EMCCA). It comprises six countries, namely Cameroon, Congo, Gabon, Equatorial Guinea, Central African Republic and Chad. As for Senegal, it is a member of the Economic Community of West African States (ECOWAS) which includes eight countries, namely Benin, Burkina Faso, Cote d'Ivoire, Mali and Senegal.

simultaneously, we propose to analyze the relationship between formality and frequency of innovation. So this paper aims to provide answers to the following research questions:

RQ1. How formality affect product, process, organizational or commercial SME innovation?
RQ2. What effect formality has on SME frequency innovation?

To answer these questions, the objective of this paper is therefore to examine the relationship between formality and innovation of SME in Cameroon and Senegal.

The data used come from IRDC as part of the project on the determinants of business performance in ASF. We use binomial logit model to evaluate the role of formality to the capacity of SME to develop product, process, commercial or organizational innovation and other hand multinomial regression to study the effect of formality to the capacity of SME to develop simultaneous different types of innovation. The results show that formality significantly determines the capacity of SME innovation. Besides, the role of formality varies depending on the type of innovation, the sector of activity, and the country.

The rest of the paper is organized as follows. Section 2 presents a review of the literature. Section 3 is devoted to the data and methodology of the study. Section 4 presents the results and interpretations. Section 5 concludes.

2. Literature review

A very recent empirical literature analyzes the impact of the coexistence of the formal sector and the informal sector on the capacity to innovate companies in developing countries. The results of this literature present two main strands.

The first shows intuitively that the coexistence in the same economy of the informal and formal sectors is harmful to business innovation [28]. Indeed, according to Mendi and Mudida [25], informal status negatively affects the innovation-decision of firms. Thus the marginal impact of informality on the innovation of formal enterprises decreases with the intensity of competitive pressure from informal enterprises. In this sense [29] highlight an inverted U-shaped relationship between the propensity to innovate and the competitive pressure of companies in the informal sector. For Ref. [30], this informal competition harms the innovation of formal companies. For Ref. [28] this negative impact is more noticeable at the level of product innovation and the most affected firms are those that lack a collaborative strategy with informal companies. According to Ref. [13], the start of the innovation-decision derives from the fact that informal enterprises provide low-quality products compared to those offered by formal enterprises since they share the same market. In this context, the low-income levels of consumers lead them to prefer low-quality products making it unprofitable for formal firms that offer superior quality products. For Ref. [31] it is the limitation on access to factors of production, especially human capital that is called into question. Indeed, the predominance of the informal sector in the economy distorts the accumulation of human capital, because the immediate availability of jobs requiring low qualifications in the informal sector, can discourage the accumulation of human capital, which makes this rarer factor. Advocates of this thesis, however, have overlooked the possibilities of interaction between firms in the two sectors.

The second cleavage shows with supporting examples that this coexistence of the two formal and informal sectors is a source of innovation [32]. Indeed, it leads to collaborations to innovate between firms [33]. For [34] the rapid democratization of innovation leads both consumers and companies to share information on the development of new products. This democratization of innovation is made possible by crowdfunding financing, which thus resolves the thorny problem of access to corporate finance [35]. Links Mhula et al. [36] show that the interaction between actors in rural areas in South Africa leads formal companies to develop innovations so the characteristics are similar to informal innovations. For Wiliams and Kosta [37], formal firms that do not perceive informal competition as an obstacle significantly increase their market shares than those which see this competition as an obstacle. Informal competition thus becomes a factor in boosting the innovation efforts of formal enterprises to cope with the rise of the informal sector. For Avenyo et al. [28], it is more intra-industry competition that improves product innovation. However, these authors show that local competition affects the product innovation strategies of large firms less than those of medium-sized firms. Based on the above arguments on the positive impact of formality on firms' innovation, we formulate the following hypothesis:

H1. The impact of formality on each type of innovation (product, process, organizational or commercial) is positive in SME.
H2. Simultaneously investing in different forms of innovation (frequency innovation) is positive related to formality in the all firm size.

It emerges from this review that although SME are very exposed to competition from the informal sector, the effect of this sectoral duality in developing economies on business innovation remains to be determined. As this effect can differentiate the degree of the economic integration of countries, this study, therefore, aims to contribute by taking the example of two countries belonging to two different economic unions.

3. Methodology

3.1 Data and variable measures

The empirical analysis of this study uses data collected as part of the Determinants of FSA Firm Performance Project funded by IDRC. As in Cameroon, data collection in Senegal was carried out based on the general census of enterprises and surveys undertaken among the informal sector. Thus, our sample is made up of both informal and formal enterprises. An informal enterprise is an enterprise that does not keep accounts according to regulations, does not pay employees' social contributions, and does not file statistical tax returns.

After analysis and processing of the data, in particular the missing data, we have a total sample of 1369, i.e. 642 in Cameroon and 727 in Senegal. **Table 1** in the appendix shows the distribution of firms. It appears that the sample is made up of 59.82% of very small enterprises (VSE), 14.90% of small enterprises (SE), 10.08% of medium-sized enterprises (ME), and 15.19% of large enterprises. (LE). Depending on the formality, 68.22% of Cameroonian businesses are informal and 31.78% formal against

60.11% informal and 39.89% formal in Senegal. The breakdown by sector of activity shows that 23.05% of Cameroonian companies are in the industrial sector against 29.99% in Senegal. Unlike Cameroon, where we find 46.11% of companies in the services, Senegal has 29.16%. In commerce, Senegalese companies are more important than in Cameroon with 38.65% against 29.60%.

By innovation surveys carried out around the world (CIS survey), firms were questioned on four main forms of innovation, namely product, process, organizational and commercial innovations. Thus, we estimate the probability for each company to develop each of these innovations on the one hand and the probability of implementing several forms of innovation on the other hand. From Chart 1 in the appendix, it emerges that it is commercial innovation which is the first form of innovation (46.11%) developed in Cameroon, while it is the last in Senegal (29.30%). The analysis according to the formality highlights a better capacity of informal enterprises to develop product innovations (30.99% in Cameroon and 19.80% in Senegal) and commercial (21.96% in Cameroon and 20.49% in Senegal). As for formal Cameroonian firms, they are more oriented towards organizational innovations (27.57%) and commercial (35.78); while formal Senegalese companies innovate the most in the process (23.19%) and organization (22.55%).

Table 2 in the appendix presents the description of the study variables. The probability of innovating is explained by two models. In the first model, where we explain the probability of the company to innovate in a product, process, marketing or organization each of the variables to be explained is binary. These variables were constructed based on a set of questions asked to firms. For product innovation, companies were asked were some of your product innovations introduced between 2011 and 2013 new to your market, or new to your business. Or significantly improved? For process innovations, between 2011 and 2013, did your company introduce any new features or significant improvements concerning your manufacturing processes? Your logistics methods? Your support or support activities? For organizational innovations, the question was whether between 2011 and 2013, the firm introduced innovations relating to new operating methods for the organization of procedures, new methods of work organization, and decision-making, external relations with other companies or organizations. Finally, for commercial innovations, it was asked whether between 2011 and 2013, the firm introduced marketing innovations relating to significant changes in the presentation of a product, the use of new techniques or new media for the promotion of products, significant new methods of selling or distribution or new pricing strategies for their products.

As for the probability of implementing several innovations, the distribution of this variable (frequency of innovation) shows that firms belong to five groups: those not innovating at all, those who innovate in one form of innovation, those developing two forms of innovation, those which implement three forms and those which manage to develop the four forms of innovation.

The explanatory variables group together the characteristics of the firm, in particular the location, size, number of employees, age, ICT [38, 39]. Besides, we have associated with the manager's characteristics, namely: gender, marital status, religious affiliation, level of education, technical training, and age group [40, 41]. We have introduced the sectoral indicators which allow us to capture the specificities linked to each sector of activity of the company **Table 3** in the appendix presents the descriptive statistics of the different variables.

3.2 Methods

Concerning the nature of the variables to be explained (binary and categorical), we use two different estimation techniques.

3.2.1 Effect of formality on firm innovation

The objective is to distinguish firms that have innovated from others, the dependent variable is dichotomous. It takes the value 1 when the company innovates and the value 0 otherwise. This is why the binomial logit is used to estimate the probability of innovating. Let π be the firm's decision to innovate, $\pi_i = 1$ if there is innovation and $\pi_i = 0$ if not. The prediction made through this model makes it possible to quantify the strength of the link between the explanatory variables and the explained variable representing the propensity to innovate [42]. The technique thus adopted does not impose restrictions on the conditions of normality of the explanatory variables, nor does it impose any restrictions on the discrete nature or not of these variables. We can therefore admit that the diversified nature of the explanatory variables, the hypothesis of the non-linearity of the relationship between the decision to innovate and the explanatory variables characterizing it, as well as the recognized flexibility of the logistics models, justify the option taken here to study the relationship between formality and the propensity to innovate.

We assume that a firm's decision to innovate is a function of the likely use of its experiences in innovating. Let π the latent variable representing the firm's propensity to innovate vary from $-\infty$ to $+\infty$. This variable is determined by explanatory variables describing the specificities of the innovation so that we have the following equation:

$$\pi^* = \alpha + X_i\beta + \varepsilon_i \tag{1}$$

Where $i$indicate the observation, $\beta$is the vector of parameters to be estimated, X the matrix of independent variables, and the error term, εwhich asymptotically follows a normal distribution.

By considering that the probable utility of innovating is $U_A(\pi\ )$ and the probable utility of not innovating is $U_N(\pi\ )$ and the latent variable is π^*, we have:

$$\pi_i = \begin{cases} 1\ if\ \pi^* > 0\ or\ U_A(\pi^*) > U_N(\pi^*) \\ 0\ if\ \pi^* < 0\ or\ U_A(\pi^*) < U_N(\pi^*) \end{cases} \tag{2}$$

In our case, the utility of innovating $U\ (\pi^*)$ is assumed to be related to all of the specific characteristics of the innovation and of the company as defined in Eq. (1). These are the characteristics of the company, the characteristics of the manager to which we associate the sector indicators. Therefore, the probability that a company innovates, for a given value of x can be expressed as follows:

$$\Pr(\pi = 1/x) = \Pr(\pi^* > 0/x) \tag{3}$$

By integrating the structural model obtained in Eq. (1) into Eq. (3) and by rearranging the terms, the probability of innovating by a company becomes:

DOI: http://dx.doi.org/10.5772/intechopen.101738

$$\Pr(1/x) = \Pr(\varepsilon > -(\alpha + \beta x)) \tag{4}$$

Thus, the empirical model used to estimate the probability of innovating takes the form:

$$Prob\ inno = \log\left(\frac{P_i}{1-P_i}\right) = \beta_0 + \beta_1 formality\_en_i + \sum_{k=2}^{K} \beta_k Z_i + \text{ssect\_act}_i + \varepsilon_i \tag{5}$$

Where $\frac{P_i}{1-P_i}$ is the ratio between the probability that a company i innovates and the probability that it does not innovate. Our variable of interest $formality\_en_i$ corresponds to whether the firm is formal or not. Z_i is the vector of control variables that groups together the characteristics of the firm and the manager. Also, sectoral indicators are introduced. ε_i the error term comprising all the variables that can explain the probability of innovating and which have not been considered here. Finally, it should be noted that Eq. (5) is estimated for each type of innovation, namely product, process, organizational, and commercial.

3.2.2 Effect of formality on firm frequency innovation

To analyze the role of formality on the frequency of innovation, we use a multinomial logit model. It is a model that conceptualizes utilities in terms of a firm's likelihood of developing some form of innovation. Thus, the choice of a form of innovation j depends on the gain in terms of utility that the firm achieves compared to other forms of innovation. Thus, the firm to make a choice ranks the utility functions of all categories of innovation and chooses the highest one. The utility of modality j depends on company γ_i and takes the form:

$$U_j = X_j\beta + \varepsilon_i \tag{6}$$

In other words, modeling a choice j for a company n in $m+1$ modalities takes form:

$$\begin{aligned} prob\ (y_n = j) &= p(u_j > u_0, u_j > u_1 \dots u_j > u_k > u_m) \\ &= p(X_{nj}\beta + \varepsilon_j > X_{nk}\beta + \varepsilon_k)\ for\ k \neq j\ and\ k = 0, 1, \dots. \\ &= p(\varepsilon_j - \varepsilon_k > X_{nk}\beta - X_{nj}\beta) \\ &= p\left(\varepsilon_j^* > X_j^*\right) \text{with, } \varepsilon_j^* = \varepsilon_j - \varepsilon_k \text{et, } X_j^* = X_k - X_j. \end{aligned} \tag{7}$$

Considering Eq. (14), the probability becomes:

$$prob\ (y_n = j) = \frac{\exp\left(X_{nj}\beta_j\right)}{\sum_{k=0}^{m} \exp\left(X_{nk}\beta_j\right)} \tag{8}$$

Avec, $n = 1, 2, 3 \dots N, number\ of\ firms\ and\ k = 1, 2, 3 \dots m,$ choices.
By normalizing by $\beta_0 = 0$, we get:

$$prob\,(y_n = j) = \frac{\exp\left(X_{nj}\beta_j\right)}{1 + \sum_{k=1}^{m} \exp\left(X_{nk}\beta_j\right)} \tag{9}$$

By considering that the parameters of this model are interpreted as a difference of β_0 from the reference modality, we obtain:

$$prob\,(y_n = j) = \frac{\frac{\exp\left(X_{nj}\beta_j\right)}{\exp\left(X_n\beta_0\right)}}{\sum_{k=1}^{m} \frac{\exp\left(X_{nk}\beta_k\right)}{\exp\left(X_n\beta_0\right)}} \tag{10}$$

$$prob\,(y_n = j) = \frac{\exp\left(X_n\left(\beta_j - \beta_0\right)\right)}{\sum_{k=1}^{m}(X_n(\beta_k - \beta_0))} \tag{11}$$

$$prob\,(y_n = j) = \frac{\exp\left(X_n\beta_j^*\right)}{\sum_{k=1}^{m} \exp\left(X_n\beta_k^*\right)} \tag{12}$$

with and $\beta_j^* = \beta_j - \beta_0$ et $\beta_k^* = \beta_k - \beta_0$

The $m + 1$ the probabilities are therefore estimated as a function of $m(m + 1)/2$ differences in $\beta_k - \beta_j$. The ratio of probabilities leads to a simple linear function of the form:

$$\frac{prob(Y_n = j)}{prob(Y_n = p)} = \frac{\frac{\exp\left(X_n\beta_j\right)}{\sum_{k=0}^{m} \exp\left(X_n\beta_k\right)}}{\frac{\exp\left(X_n\beta_p\right)}{\sum_{k=0}^{m} \exp\left(X_n\beta_k\right)}} = \exp\left(X_n\left(\beta_j - \beta_p\right)\right) \tag{13}$$

Related to the logarithm, the equation results in a simple linear function:

The categorical variable frequency of innovation (freq_innov) measuring the ability to implement several forms of innovation being defined according to five modalities, the empirical equation to be estimated is written:

$$\text{freq\_innov} = P[j/X_i] = \frac{exp\left(X_i\beta_j\right)}{\sum_{h=0}^{2} exp\left(X_i\beta_h\right)} \tag{14}$$

with,

$$j = \begin{cases} 0 \text{ non} - \text{innovative firms} \\ 1 \text{ innovative firms in one form of innovation} \\ 2 \text{ innovative firms in two form} s\ of \text{ innovation} \\ 3 \text{ innovative firms in three forms of innovation} \\ 4 \text{ innovative firms in four forms of innovation} \end{cases}$$

Statistics show that since non-innovative firms are the most numerous in the base, they are considered as a reference group. Thus, we get:

$$\begin{cases} P[0/X_i] = \dfrac{1}{1+\sum_{h=1}^{2} exp\,(X_i\beta_h)}, & for\, j = 0 \\ P[j/X_i] = \dfrac{1}{1+\sum_{h=0}^{2} exp\,(X_i\beta_h)}, & for\, j = 1,2,3,4 \end{cases} \tag{15}$$

Where X_i is the vector of the explanatory variables. The final model to be estimated is as follows:

$$\text{freq\_innov} = log\left(\frac{P[j/X_i]}{P[0/X_i]}\right) = X_i\beta_j = \beta_{j0} + \beta_{j1} formality\_en_i + \sum_{k=2}^{K} \beta_{jk} Z_i + ssect\_act + \varepsilon_i \tag{16}$$

Where $s\,sec\,t\_act$ represents the sectoral indicators.

We estimate this equation using a multinomial logit whose structure allows us to determine the influence of formality on the probability of belonging to each of the categories of companies mentioned above (j = 0,1,2,3,4) compared to those having not innovated during the study period (j = 0). Note that the explained variable being an intensity variable, we also estimated the ordered model as is often the case. The results being the same, in particular the positive effect of formality on the frequency of firm innovation, we only present the results of the unordered model.

4. Results and discussions

This section presents the results obtained from the models previously presented. First, we discuss the role of formality on the propensity of firms to develop each type of innovation. Second, we discuss the relationship between formality of firm frequency of innovation. The robustness of the results has been verified using a variance inflation test (VIF) (**Table 4**).

4.1 Formal firms have a better propensity to innovate

Tables 5 and **6** in the appendix present the results of the determinants of product and process innovation as well as organizational and commercial innovations for each of the countries and the overall sample of companies. Globally, the results show a positive relationship between formality and the propensity of companies to innovate in both Cameroon and Senegal. In other words, formal enterprises compared to informal enterprises have a better capacity for innovation. Thus, the fact that a company is formal increases its probability of innovating in products by 43.86% and the process by 51.66% in Senegal against 35.85% in product and 36.16% in process in Cameroon. In contrast, when considering organizational and commercial innovations, formality increases the probability of innovating by 51.33 and 57.15% in Cameroon against 48.70 and 45.07% in Senegal respectively. When the sectors of activity are taken into account (**Tables 7–10**), formality remains an important factor in the capacity for innovation of companies, although its role is different. In the case of product innovation, we note that formal Senegalese companies have a better propensity to innovate regardless of the sector of activity. In contrast in Cameroon, formality does not seem to be a determinant of product innovation. By considering process innovation, the results attest that the formality contributes to the innovation of Cameroonian firms in the industrial and commercial sectors. In Senegal, it appears that it improves the propensity to innovate in the three sectors of activity. As for organizational innovation, formality appears to be decisive in industry and service companies in Cameroon. On the other hand in Senegal, it determines the innovation capacity of trade and service companies. Finally, about commercial innovations, the results show that formality is a determining factor in Cameroon in trade and Senegal in trade and services.

Beyond formality, our results show that several other factors contribute to the implementation of innovations within companies. In line with work carried out in Africa [43], our study shows that the size of the company is an important determinant of innovation, although its role is not systematic according to the forms of innovation. Besides, companies located in large urban centers have a better capacity for innovation. They seem to benefit from the exchange of information and collaborations with other companies in the innovation process. Also, our results show that the age of the company determines the capacity for innovation, with a more determining effect in Senegalese companies. However, we note that in the Senegalese industrial sector, its role is negative in the context of process innovations. This shows that in this sector, it is young companies that are more oriented towards innovation. We also note the important role of ICT in the innovation process in both Cameroon and Senegal. Our results also confirm the important role played by the number of employees in innovation. When taking into account the types of innovation, companies with a large number of employees exhibit a better capacity for innovation. Taking into account the sectors of activity, it emerges that the number of employees is decisive in the industry both in Cameroon and in Senegal regardless of the type of innovation. However, our results show a negative effect on the number of employees in Senegalese service companies that develop business innovations. This result thus shows that it is important for companies to emphasize the qualifications of employees, a source of innovation, and not only on the workforce, as is very often the case in French-speaking Sub-Saharan Africa.

Contrary to certain results obtained in developing countries and Africa in particular, our analysis underlines the determining role of R&D activities in the implementation of innovations in Cameroon and Senegal. Indeed, it emerges that companies that have an R&D activity have a better capacity for innovation. However, our analysis shows that the role of R&D is not systematic when we take into account the forms of innovation according to the sectors of activity. It appears that R&D seems to be decisive in the industrial sector as well as in services in Cameroon, while in Senegal R&D improves the product innovation capacity of service companies. In terms of process innovations, R&D plays an important role in service companies in Cameroon and all sectors in Senegal. Finally, by considering organizational and commercial innovations, we see that R&D is decisive mainly within service companies. Our study attests to the results obtained by Ref. [44] and shows that R&D activities must be taken into account when defining innovation policies in Africa [45]. But this must be done taking into account sector specificities insofar as R&D also plays a decisive role in service companies.

Finally, our work shows that firms that develop innovations in Africa as in other environments fundamentally rely on the characteristics of the manager as well as his qualifications and skills. In this sense, it emerges that the technical training of the manager increases the propensity of companies to innovate, with a greater effect in

Senegal. We also note the role of manager education as well as age, the sometimes negative effect of which shows that companies with young managers have a better capacity for innovation. Finally, like [46] in Tanzania, our work emphasizes that gender determines innovation.

4.2 The frequency of innovation is positively linked to the formality of the firms

The results in **Table 11** validate the idea that the frequency of innovation increases with the formality of the business. The graphs in **Figure 1** which present for the four forms of innovation the evolution of the marginal effect as a function of the formality of the firm attest to the positive relationship between the formality of the firm and the observed innovation capacity previously. In the case of Cameroon, the fact that a company is formal increases its frequency of developing innovation by 14.60, 23.11% for two forms, 15.35% for three forms, and 18.69% for the four forms of innovation. As for Senegal, formality increases the frequency of innovating by 22.96% for one form, by 21.38% for two forms, by 13.62% for three forms, and by 19.40% for all four forms innovation. However, we see that this increase is less significant in Cameroon when the company develops from three forms of innovation.

The results in **Table 11** validate the idea that the frequency of innovation increases with the formality of the firm. The graphs in **Figure 1**, which show the evolution of the marginal effect as a function of firm formality for the four forms of innovation, attest to the positive relationship between firm formality and innovation capacity observed earlier. In the case of Cameroon, the fact that a company is formal increases its frequency of developing an innovation by 14.60, 23.11% for two forms, 15.35% for three forms and 18.69% for all four forms of innovation. As for Senegal, formality increases the frequency of innovation by 22.96% for one form, 21.38% for two forms, 13.62% for three forms and 19.40% for all four forms of innovation. However, this increase is less significant in Cameroon when the company develops from three forms of innovation.

The results by sector of activity (**Tables 12–14**) confirm those previously obtained, in particular, that formality positively affects companies' propensity to innovate. However, we note that the relationship between formality and frequency of innovation is more decisive in the case of Senegalese companies.

In the industrial sector, formality improves the innovation capacity of Cameroonian companies which develop three and four forms of innovation. In Senegal, on the other hand, formality contributes to the propensity to innovate, both for companies that implement one or two forms of innovation and for those adopting three and four forms of innovation. In commercial enterprises, formality remains very decisive in the capacity for innovation of Senegalese companies. The results show that formality systematically impacts the frequency of innovation. In Cameroon, on the other hand, formality is only decisive for companies that adopt two types of innovation. Finally, in service companies, we see that formality is a factor of innovation. In Cameroon, it impacts the frequency of innovation of companies that develop two and three forms of innovation, while in Senegal, its role remains decisive for all forms of innovation.

The analysis of the other characteristics confirms the results obtained in the case of the different facets of innovation because it appears that the frequency of innovation depends on several factors. First, we observe that R&D improves the frequency of innovation only in Senegalese companies that implement at least two forms of innovation. This result suggests that despite resource constraints, companies consider it important to invest in improving manufacturing processes in support or support

Cameroon

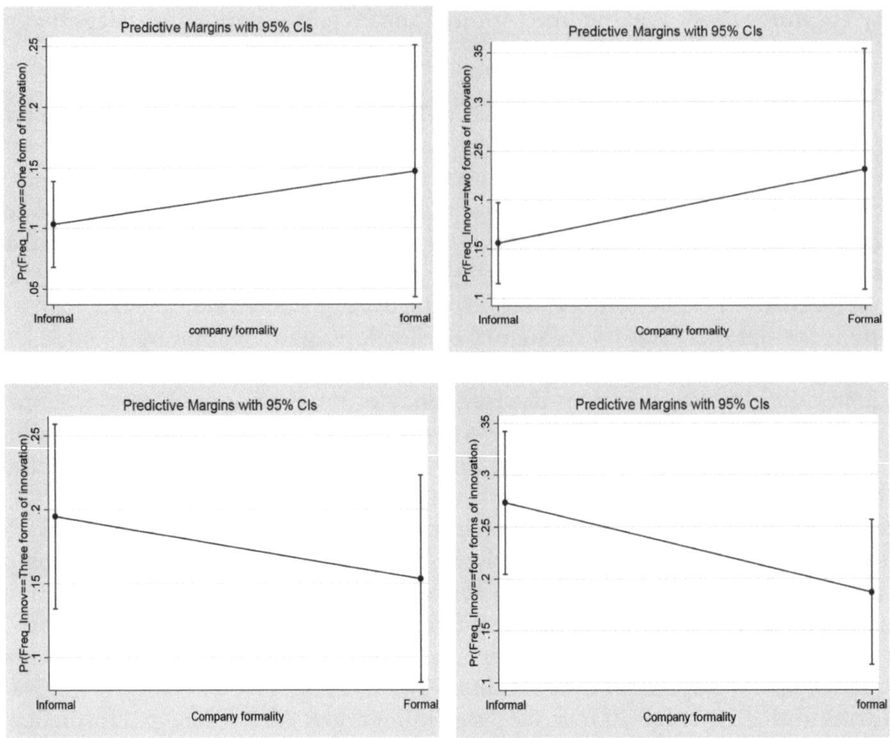

Senegal

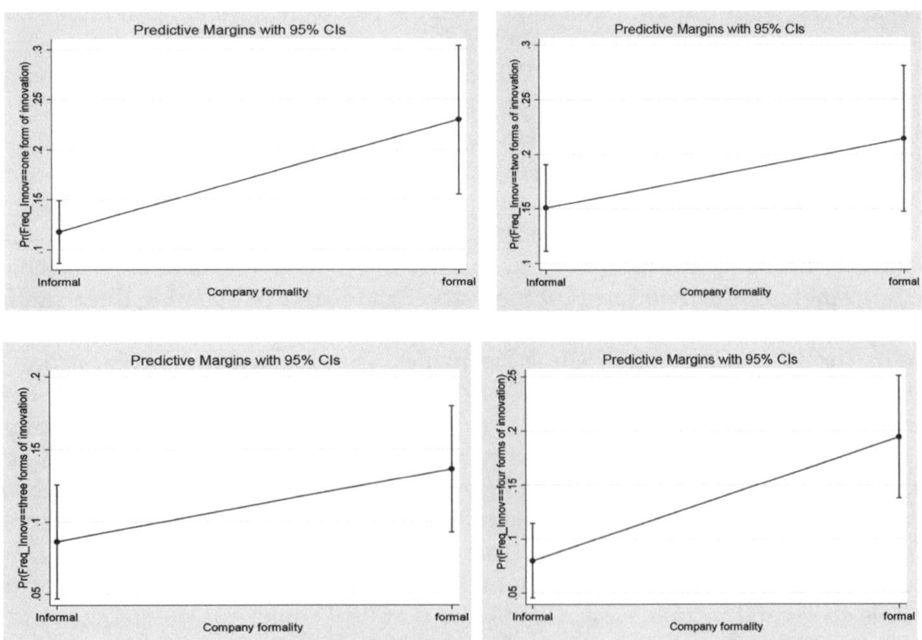

Figure 1.
Marginal effects of formality on the probability of innovating.

activities as well as logistics to hope to take advantage of the benefits and spinoffs related to this form of innovation, the impact of which is generally considerable [47]. Senegalese companies seem to be part of a dynamic contrary to that observed in the economies of the Maghreb since the work carried out in this context [48] shows that R&D is not a determining variable in the innovation process. Our analyzes, therefore, show that it is relevant to take into account forms of innovation rather than considering an aggregate measure of innovation.

In addition, we note that companies located in large urban centers have a better frequency of innovation. We also note that size plays a determining role. In the case of Cameroon, its role is decisive for companies that adopt at least three forms of innovation. In contrast, in Senegal, it improves the frequency of innovation for small businesses that adopt at most two forms of innovation as well as for medium and large businesses that develop at least two forms of innovation. The results also show that the number of employees improves the frequency of innovation, and we observe in the case of Senegal that its impact is more decisive for young companies that set up a single form of innovation. In addition, our analyses show that age and ICT improve the frequency of innovation. Like [49] in Nigeria, our analyses highlight the key role of manager characteristics in the capacity for innovation. It appears that the manager's gender, level of education, age, and religious affiliation determines the frequency of innovation. Finally, the analysis according to the activity sectors also highlights the impact of the afore mentioned characteristics on the frequency of innovation with some important specificities. Particularly concerning the role of R&D.

4.3 Discussion

Our results generally show that there is a positive relationship between formality and business innovation. Indeed, it has been established that formality increases the innovation capacity of enterprises on the one hand and that informal enterprises have a low frequency of innovation on the other. These results thus reinforce the work in Africa which has shown that the productive fabric in this context is heterogeneous, marked by a formal and informal divide and therefore a better understanding of this duality can help boost business productivity and economic growth.

In the specific case of analyzes on innovation factors, our analyses essentially confirm the results obtained in Kenya by Mendi and Mudida [25] and Fu et al., [26] in Ghana. Mendi and Mudida [25] find that the fact that a business starts up informal has a low impact on its capacity for innovation. As for Fu et al. [26] in Ghana, they attest that formal companies have a better capacity for innovation, particularly about technological innovations and better productivity. Following on from them, our analyzes confirm this relationship even in the case of organizational and commercial innovations. We thus show that, if non-technological innovation in a dual productive fabric dominated by SMEs as is the case in Cameroon and Senegal, is strongly based on the manager's qualifications and skills, on the other hand, the formalization of companies is essential because it gives access to qualified employees, to information and exchanges with other companies. In addition, our work attests to considerable sectoral differences since it is demonstrated that formality further increases the capacity for innovation in the industry, then in services, and slightly in trading companies.

Unlike the analyzes of Agwu et al. [50] whose work on African countries shows that there are no differences between countries in innovation trends within companies, we show that even if overall the innovation factors tend to be the same, on the other hand, it is important to carry out comparative studies between countries, especially when the latter belong to different economic zones. Indeed, it has turned out that R&D is a much more important factor in Senegalese companies, especially in the industrial and service sectors. In addition, Senegalese companies have a higher frequency of innovation insofar as they develop several innovations. This result shows that formalization promotes access to information through the collaborations that companies develop and allows them to favor complementarity in terms of innovations rather than substitution, which is a much more expensive process for small businesses firms. From this perspective, R&D seems to be an essential asset.

Finally, we show that the frequency of business innovation increases with formality. This result which is established in the two countries with a strong significance in Senegal shows that one way to improve the rate and the scale of the innovation of the companies being able to make it possible to reach the visions of development fixed by the two countries is the formalization of companies. Indeed, so far, innovations in business in Africa appear to be minor and adaptive. And very often the result of managers. Certainly, in recent years, policies have been adopted to facilitate the formalization of businesses, but surveys show that informal businesses remain very predominant in the productive fabric and that the two countries (Cameroon in particular) have changed very little in the doing business ranking. In Senegal, for example, despite the process of formalization and business support initiated by the International Labor Office and government authorities, we note that 9 out of ten workers are in informal employment [51].

5. Conclusion and recommendations

Business formalization and innovation remain major concerns in ASF's economies. Indeed, the productive fabric in this space remains dominated by informal businesses, limited access to quality human resources, a low-incentive business climate, and very limited access to financing their activities. In such a context, understanding the role of formality in the innovation process appears essential in the face of the challenges of development and survival of companies but also in the context of the definition of public innovation policies. Research has shown that formal enterprises are not only the most likely to adopt and develop innovations, but also have better economic performance. Thus, the objective of this article was to analyze the relationship between formality and innovation in companies in Cameroon and Senegal. In particular, we have studied the role of formality on the capacity for innovation but also the frequency of innovation. Our results thus aim to provide a better understanding of this relationship in the context of French-speaking African countries which for the majority are oriented towards growth strategies (Plan Senegal Emergent, 2035 and Growth Strategy for Employment, 2035 for Cameroon).

Our results show that in this space, formality improves the innovation capacity of companies. Much more, it determines the frequency of innovation with greater effect in Senegal and industrial and service companies. Moreover, we have found that business characteristics including age, location, size, ICT, number of employees improve the capacity and frequency of business innovation. In addition, our analyzes have shown that it is important to continue R&D activities since the industrial and service companies that carry out their activities have a better frequency of innovation. Finally, our results confirmed the major role of manager characteristics and skills in the innovation process.

It is therefore essential to intensify initiatives aimed at the formalization of businesses if we want to promote the development of innovations in French-speaking Africa and move from simple copying of innovations and their adaptation to real innovations that can impact growth. On this issue, Cameroonian public authorities are even more concerned because not only does the rate of informality remain very high in Cameroon, but the impact of formality remains insignificant, especially when considering the frequency of innovation. It, therefore, seems essential not to be limited to accompanying measures towards formalization. Indeed, to move towards the objective of industrialization, Senegal and Cameroon must further promote incentive frameworks that would allow companies to legalize and formalize their activities. Certainly, several measures have already been developed and others are underway, but their impact remains mixed given the weight that the informal sector still represents. Studies on obstacles to the formalization of companies could lead to more appropriate policies.

Therefore, if we want to boost the rate of innovation, the process of supporting businesses towards formalization must emphasize measures aimed at supporting them financially. Such initiatives would allow companies to reduce the financial constraints linked to the formalization process. These measures are essential and would benefit more the small informal enterprises which are experiencing real cash flow problems. States can also go towards incentives for small businesses that decide to regularize their activities.

As it is considered difficult to put an end to informal activities, government authorities must therefore give greater importance to informal enterprises since their actions force formal enterprises to more innovation. The public authorities could perhaps imagine a model of collaboration between formal and informal enterprises which would allow developing more innovation and thus boost performance and growth and would cause informal enterprises to regularize. Finally, an important emphasis must be placed on employee training. Indeed, our results have shown that the number of employees determines the innovation capacity of companies. In this sense, companies must place significant emphasis on training them to develop their skills and thus take advantage of the opportunities in their environment to develop more innovations.

Acknowledgements

The authors thank Ms Beyala Marie for her comments and suggestions.

Appendix

Designation		Cameroon					Senegal				
		Number of firm	Innovative product firms	Innovative process firms	Innovative firms in organization	Innovative marketing firms	Number of firm	Innovative product firms	Innovative process firms	Innovative firms in organization	Innovative marketing firms
Firm size	VSE	394	200	188	201	222	425	139	137	116	103
	SE	67	29	32	33	42	137	44	56	61	42
	ME	55	22	25	26	35	83	26	28	34	29
	LE	126	52	51	59	61	82	34	45	42	39
firm formality	Formal	204	104	118	177	219	437	130	167	164	64
	Informal	438	199	178	142	141	290	144	99	89	149
Sector of activity	Industry	148	80	90	79	91	218	91	87	68	53
	Commerce	198	78	66	77	98	281	85	81	86	77
	Service	296	141	136	159	168	212	66	91	92	78

Table 1.
Description of the sample.

Variable	Définitions
Dependent variables	
in_produ	Binary variable equal to 1 if the firm declares to have innovated a product and 0 if not.
in_proce	Binary variable equal to 1 if the firm declares to have innovated in process and 0 if not.
in_orga	Binary variable equal to 1 if the firm declares to have developed an organizational innovation and 0 if not.
in_come	Binary variable equal to 1 if the firm declares to have developed a business innovation and 0 if not.
freq_innov	Categorical variable equal to 0 for non-innovative firms, to 1 for firms that have developed only one form of innovation, to 2 for two forms, to 1 for three forms and to 4 for all four forms.
Explanatory variables	
Formality_en	Binary variable equal to 1 if the firm is formal and 0 if not.
localisation	Binary variable equal to 1 if the firm is located in an urban center and 0 if not.
r_dev	Binary variable equal to 1 if the firm carries out R&D activities and 0 if not.
Lage	Logarithm of the age of the firm
taille_ent	Categorical variable equal to 0 for very small enterprises (VSE), 1 for small enterprises (SE), 2 for medium enterprises (ME) and 3 for large enterprises (LE)
Tic	Binary variable equal to 1 if the firm has at least one tick equipment and 0 if not.
Leffec	Logarithm of the number of employees

Variable	Définitions
Ltic	Logarithm of the number of ict equipment in the firm
tranche_age	Manager's age group
instruc_ma	Categorical variable equal to 0 for managers with no formal education, 1 for those with primary education, 2 for secondary (2) and 3 for higher.
sex_ma	Binary variable equal to 1 if the manager is male 0 if not.
fortec_ma	Binary variable equal to 1 if the manager has a technical training related to the main activity of the company and 0 if not.
relig_ma	Categorical variable equal to 0 for animist managers, equal to 1 for Muslim managers, equal to 2 for Catholics, equal to 3 for Protestants and equal to 4 for other Christians.
stat_ma	Categorical variable equal to 0 for widowed managers, equal to 1 for single managers, equal to 2 for divorced managers and equal to 3 for married managers.

Table 2.
Description of variables.

Variables	Observations	Mean	Standard deviation
in_produ	1369	0.3995617	0.0132429
in_proce	1369	0.4105186	0.0133002
in_orga	1369	0.4178232	0.0133346
in_come	1369	0.4185537	0.0133379
freq_innov	1369	1.646457	0.0413806
r_dev	1369	0.0759679	0.0071633
formality_en	1369	0.3608473	0.0129844
localisation	1369	0.8071585	0.0106669
taille_ent	1369	0.806428	0.0304609
leffec	1369	1.778067	0.0444247
tic	1369	0.6639883	0.0127707
lage	1369	2.363425	0.0194964
ltic	1369	1.233775	0.0226089
sex_ma	1369	0.7998539	0.0108177
stat_ma	1369	2.352082	0.0268715
relig_ma	1369	1.517896	0.0249713
instruc_ma	1369	1.719503	0.0297926
fortec_ma	1369	0.5617239	0.0134151
tranche_age	1369	0.8239591	0.03189

Table 3.
Descriptive statistics for variables.

	Cameroun			Senegal	
Variable	**VIF**	**1/VIF**	**Variables**	**VIF**	**1/VIF**
Lage	4.71	0.129740	Lage	4.22	0.236735
tranche_age	4.7	0.140963	tranche_age	3.77	0.265563
formality_en	4.76	0.210199	formality_en	2.46	0.407226
leffec	4.49	0.222811	Leffec	1.75	0.570786
Ltic	1.47	0.679462	instruc_ma	1.73	0.576618
Tic	1.47	0.680618	Ltic	1.58	0.633923
instruc_ma	1.29	0.772606	taille_ent	1.30	0.772003
sex_ma	1.14	0.879130	r_dev	1.28	0.782305
fortec_ma	1.12	0.896573	stat_ma	1.23	0.815709
r_dev	1.1	0.910413	localisation	1.16	0.862589
relig_ma	1.07	0.936015	sex_ma	1.14	0.874633
stat_ma	1.05	0.948345	fortec_ma	1.13	0.886794
localisation	1.05	0.954916	tic_a	1.12	0.893054
taille_ent	1.02	0.979067	relig_ma	1.10	0.905723

Table 4.
Multi-collinearity test of the variables.

	Product innovation			Process innovation		
Variables	**Cameroon**	**Senegal**	**Full sample**	**Cameroon**	**Senegal**	**Full sample**
r_dev	1.159***	1.165***	1.216***	1.937***	0.964**	1.588***
	(0.348)	(0.353)	(0.240)	(0.421)	(0.396)	(0.282)
formality_en	0.691*	0.870***	0.170**	0.707*	1.197***	0.433**
	(0.395)	(0.256)	(0.192)	(0.403)	(0.254)	(0.193)
localisation	1.255***		0.537***	0.981***		0.419***
	(0.311)		(0.159)	(0.309)		(0.161)
VSE		0.274**	0.307*			
		(0.228)	(0.170)			
ME		0.443*	0.364*		0.588**	
		(0.290)	(0.203)		(0.300)	
LE	0.383*					
	(0.218)					
Leffec	0.258***	0.152**	0.0878*	0.377***	0.335***	0.206***
	(0.0939)	(0.0760)	(0.0509)	(0.0983)	(0.0788)	(0.0527)
Tic			0.308**		0.0653**	0.363***
			(0.134)		(0.262)	(0.138)
lage			0.287*			

	Product innovation			Process innovation		
Variables	**Cameroon**	**Senegal**	**Full sample**	**Cameroon**	**Senegal**	**Full sample**
			(0.166)			
Ltic	0.410**		0.250***			0.157*
	(0.176)		(0.0834)			(0.0857)
sex_ma	0.327*					
	(0.193)					
stat_ma						
relig_ma			0.123*			
			(0.0662)			
instruc_ma		0.325***		0.193*		0.171***
		(0.0919)		(0.108)		(0.0650)
fortec_ma		0.784***	0.285**		0.503***	
		(0.183)	(0.120)		(0.183)	
tranche_age			−0.248**		−0.284**	−0.298***
			(0.0974)		(0.135)	(0.0998)
Constant	−1.781*	−2.372***	−2.035***	−1.714*	−2.719***	−2.017***
	(0.995)	(0.588)	(0.407)	(1.012)	(0.602)	(0.417)
Observations	642	727	1369	642	727	1369

Standard errors in parentheses.
$^{*}p < 0.1$.
$^{**}p < 0.05$.
$^{***}p < 0.01$.

Table 5.
Estimation of the probability of product and process innovation.

	Organizational innovation			Marketing innovation		
Variables	**Cameroon**	**Senegal**	**Full sample**	**Cameroon**	**Senegal**	**Full sample**
r_dev	1.369***	1.289***	1.362***	1.196***	0.684*	1.065***
	(0.402)	(0.403)	(0.280)	(0.398)	(0.352)	(0.257)
formality_en		1.086***	0.708***		1.378***	0.678***
		(0.253)	(0.195)		(0.268)	(0.197)
localisation	1.213***		0.551***	1.202***		0.598***
	(0.313)		(0.164)	(0.291)		(0.165)
PE		0.643***				
		(0.226)				
ME						
GE	0.281**			0.396*		
	(0.228)			(0.221)		
leffec	0.338***	0.190**	0.170***	0.258***	0.257***	0.132**

	Organizational innovation			Marketing innovation		
Variables	**Cameroon**	**Senegal**	**Full sample**	**Cameroon**	**Senegal**	**Full sample**
	(0.102)	(0.0783)	(0.0534)	(0.0996)	(0.0825)	(0.0535)
tic			0.307**			0.590***
			(0.140)			(0.140)
lage						
ltic	0.130**					
	(0.180)					
sex_ma						
stat_ma			0.110*		0.239**	0.195***
			(0.0637)		(0.119)	(0.0635)
relig_ma				0.0414**		0.202***
				(0.0825)		(0.0682)
instruc_ma			0.211***			0.243***
			(0.0659)			(0.0664)
fortec_ma					0.395**	
					(0.197)	
tranche_age						−0.198**
						(0.101)
Constant	−2.071**	−2.038***	−1.956***	−0.177***	−1.999***	−1.886***
	(1.026)	(0.590)	(0.424)	(1.014)	(0.617)	(0.426)
Observations	642	727	1369	642	727	1369

Standard errors in parentheses.
$^{*}p < 0.1$.
$^{**}p < 0.05$.
$^{***}p < 0.01$.

Table 6.
Estimation of the probability of organizational and marketing innovation.

	Cameroon			Senegal		
Variables	**Industry**	**Trade**	**Service**	**Industry**	**Trade**	**Service**
r_dev	2.838**	1.776**	0.878*			1.482***
	(1.272)	(0.868)	(0.450)			(0.536)
formality_en				1.304**	1.278***	1.112**
				(0.660)	(0.444)	(0.509)
localisation	1.804***	1.550**	0.903*	0.312***	0.331**	0.0301***
	(0.612)	(0.643)	(0.503)	(0.561)	(0.336)	(0.405)

	Cameroon			Senegal		
Variables	**Industry**	**Trade**	**Service**	**Industry**	**Trade**	**Service**
VSE						
ME	1.453*					
	(0.782)					
LE	0.815***	0.871**		0.500**	0.911*	
	(0.518)	(0.421)		(0.657)	(0.530)	
leffec	0.233***		0.325**	0.778***	0.552***	
	(0.197)		(0.134)	(0.211)	(0.157)	
tic		0.365**	0.0377***	0.293**	0.506*	0.933*
		(0.389)	(0.334)	(0.624)	(0.447)	(0.532)
lage				0.0425***	0.262**	
				(0.534)	(0.403)	
ltic	0.691*	0.571*	0.280***	0.214*	0.0954***	0.172**
	(0.410)	(0.311)	(0.293)	(0.289)	(0.205)	(0.199)
sex_ma			0.603**		0.909*	
			(0.284)		(0.476)	
stat_ma		0.251*				
		(0.151)				
relig_ma						
instruc_ma	0.0849**		0.0643**	0.412**		
	(0.273)		(0.150)	(0.199)		
fortec_ma				1.328***		0.832**
				(0.500)		(0.389)
tranche_age						
Constant	−0.327**	−4.264**	−1.426	−3.594**	−2.957***	−2.838**
	(2.293)	(2.072)	(1.447)	(1.435)	(1.133)	(1.165)
Observations	148	190	296	218	281	212

Standard errors in parentheses.
$^{*}p < 0.1$.
$^{**}p < 0.05$.
$^{***}p < 0.01$.

Table 7.
Estimation of the probability of product innovation by industry sector.

	Cameroon			Senegal		
Variables	**Industry**	**Commerce**	**Service**	**Industry**	**Commerce**	**Service**
r_dev			1.839***	1.475*	2.605**	1.670**
			(0.545)	(0.857)	(1.126)	(0.709)
formality_en	0.129**	0.1638**		1.211**	0.794*	2.616***
	(0.868)	(0.325)		(0.583)	(0.422)	(0.551)
localisation	1.408**	0.755*	1.004*			
	(0.579)	(0.618)	(0.544)			
SE				0.208**	0.859**	
				(0.442)	(0.377)	
ME				0.401***	0.143***	
				(0.621)	(0.476)	
LE	0.451**	−0.845*		0.745**	0.833*	
	(0.513)	(0.450)		(0.617)	(0.504)	
Leffec	0.185***		0.394***	0.219**	0.292**	0.0737***
	(0.200)		(0.145)	(0.165)	(0.147)	(0.148)
tic						
lage				−0.677*		
				(0.406)		
ltic	0.294*	0.553*	0.279**			
	(0.416)	(0.330)	(0.317)			
sex_ma	0.314**					
	(0.486)					
stat_ma	0.335**					
	(0.170)					
relig_ma						
instruc_ma	0.279*	0.563**	0.0412*			
	(0.278)	(0.240)	(0.155)			
fortec_ma	0.00840**	0.378	−0.0695	0.0140***		
	(0.409)	(0.361)	(0.284)	(0.371)		
tranche_age						
Constant	−1.929	−2.395	−1.935	−1.176	−2.498**	−2.741**
	(2.241)	(2.159)	(1.552)	(1.125)	(1.101)	(1.181)
r_dev	−0.173	1.336	1.839***	1.475*	2.605**	(1.126)
Observations	139	190	296	218	281	212

Standard errors in parentheses.
$^{*}p < 0.1$.
$^{**}p < 0.05$.
$^{***}p < 0.01$.

Table 8.
Estimation of the probability of process innovation by industry sector.

DOI: http://dx.doi.org/10.5772/intechopen.101738

	Cameroon			Senegal		
Variables	**Industry**	**Commerce**	**Service**	**Industry**	**Commerce**	**Service**
r_dev			2.050***			
			(0.663)			
formalite_ent	0.5590758*		03653788**		1.180***	1.628***
	(0.954)		(0.314)		(0.428)	(0.486)
localisation	3.056***		0.593**			
	(0.864)		(0.480)			
SE		1.205*	0.116*			
		(0.630)	(0.481)			
ME						
LE		0.757*				
		(0.424)				
leffec	0.835***	0.323***		0.405***	0.669***	0.0324*
	(0.265)	(0.263)		(0.155)	(0.154)	(0.139)
tic	0.841*	0.239*	0.393***	0.228**	0.452*	0.196*
	(0.484)	(0.378)	(0.347)	(0.498)	(0.425)	(0.490)
lage				0.0429**	0.225*	0.509**
				(0.373)	(0.395)	(0.425)
ltic	0.535**	0.0420*	0.0763***	0.0607**	0.208***	0.202***
	(0.445)	(0.304)	(0.315)	(0.207)	(0.197)	(0.205)
sex_ma	0.343***	0.394*	0.455***			
	(0.516)	(0.374)	(0.293)			
stat_ma		0.0619**	0.308**			
		(0.153)	(0.135)			
relig_ma						
instruc_ma	−0.193***	0.508**	0.00201*			
	(0.336)	(0.223)	(0.162)			
fortec_ma	0.832*			1.031***	0.0189**	0.134**
	(0.459)			(0.371)	(0.332)	(0.363)
tranche_age				−0.0116**		
				(0.266)		
Constant	−2.291	−3.572*	−0.732	−3.161***	−2.893**	−2.712**
	(2.369)	(2.056)	(1.643)	(1.144)	(1.134)	(1.120)
Observations	148	190	296	218	281	212

Standard errors in parentheses.
$^{*}p < 0.1$.
$^{**}p < 0.05$.
$^{***}p < 0.01$.

Table 9.
Probability of organizational innovation by sector of activity.

	Cameroon			Senegal		
Variables	Industry	Commerce	Service	Industry	Commerce	Service
r_dev			1.279**		1.876*	1.061*
			(0.543)		(1.101)	(0.544)
formality_ent		1.088*			1.452***	2.001***
		(0.050)			(0.134)	(0.530)
localisation	0.0331*	1.001*	1.383***			
	(0.571)	(0.540)	(0.506)			
SE						−0.845*
						(0.458)
ME	1.121**	0.682***	0.163*			−1.030*
	(0.550)	(0.550)	(0.471)			(0.575)
GE	0.442*	−0.871**	0.0751			
	(0.235)	(0.415)	(0.347)			
leffec	0.634*	0.00762**	0.247*	0.323**	0.451***	−0.163**
	(0.461)	(0.253)	(0.143)	(0.151)	(0.147)	(0.148)
tic				0.0922***	0.187***	0.177**
				(0.479)	(0.441)	(0.509)
lage	1.021**		0.880***			
	(0.449)		(0.718)			
Ltic				0.125***	0.273*	0.192**
				(0.203)	(0.192)	(0.211)
sex_ma						
stat_ma	0.535**	0.100**				0.559**
	(0.252)	(0.152)				(0.224)
relig_ma		0.454**				
		(0.179)				
instruc_ma		0.378*		0.310*	0.305*	0.0735***
		(0.211)		(0.171)	(0.175)	(0.175)
fortec_ma				1.345***	0.373	0.822**
				(0.359)	(0.321)	(0.390)
tranche_age						
Constant	−0.559	−0.496	0.285	−3.494***	−1.882	−0.513
	(0.955)	(1.998)	(1.613)	(1.166)	(1.151)	(1.135)
Observations	139	190	296	218	281	212

Standard errors in parentheses.
$^{*}p < 0.1$.
$^{**}p < 0.05$.
$^{***}p < 0.01$.

Table 10.
Probability of marketing innovation by industry sector.

Variables	Cameroon				Senegal			
	One form	Two forms	Three forms	Four forms	One form	Two forms	Three forms	Four forms
r_dev						2.405**	2.480**	2.987***
						(1.080)	(1.072)	(1.052)
formalite_ent	0.243*	0.268**	0.496*	0.562**	1.688***	1.438***	1.610***	2.076***
	(0.692)	(0.622)	(0.623)	(0.601)	(0.364)	(0.350)	(0.422)	(0.407)
localisation	0.931**	1.780***	1.618***	1.837***	1.258***	1.019***		
	(0.434)	(0.474)	(0.461)	(0.459)	(0.318)	(0.300)		
PE					0.326*	0.391**		
					(0.341)	(0.287)		
ME						0.278*	0.501**	0.531***
						(0.398)	(0.470)	(0.442)
GE			1.012***	0.515*		0.0321***	0.427***	0.0725***
			(0.372)	(0.312)		(0.416)	(0.485)	(0.432)
leffec	0.315*	0.188**	0.547***	0.608***	−0.215*		0.484***	0.328***
	(0.177)	(0.164)	(0.157)	(0.151)	(0.118)		(0.123)	(0.119)
tic				0.261**			0.224**	0.151***
				(0.305)			(0.453)	(0.404)
lage			1.255*	0.0444**		0.521*		
			(0.672)	(0.657)		(0.294)		
ltic	0.158	0.0619**	0.269***	0.434***			0.0810***	0.255***
	(0.323)	(0.250)	(0.265)	(0.265)			(0.179)	(0.179)
sex_ma					0.625*	0.163**		
					(0.345)	(0.376)		
stat_ma								
relig_ma		0.197**				0.346*	0.290**	
		(0.126)				(0.255)	(0.283)	
instruc_ma	0.154***	0.248*	0.201***	0.0757*				
	(0.173)	(0.169)	(0.166)	(0.155)				
fortec_ma			0.0254*	0.0745***			0.559*	0.951***
			(0.273)	(0.257)			(0.299)	(0.298)
tranche_age						−0.626***		
						(0.226)		
Constant	−1.764	−3.252**	−0.576	−2.831*	−1.555*	−3.766***	−4.284***	−3.253***
	(1.686)	(1.565)	(1.555)	(1.525)	(0.803)	(0.845)	(0.987)	(0.903)
Observations	642	642	642	642	727	727	727	727

Standard errors in parentheses.
**p < 0.1.*
***p < 0.05.*
****p < 0.01.*

Table 11.
Estimation of the multinomial logit model.

Variables	Cameroon				Senegal			
	One form	Two forms	Three forms	Four forms	One form	Two forms	Three forms	Four forms
r_dev			−4.334**	−1.817*				
			(1.936)	(1.001)				
formality_en			1.040***	1.252***	1.763**	0.151***	0.996**	1.718*
			(1.379)	(1.229)	(0.854)	(0.820)	(0.913)	(0.939)
localisation	2.993***	3.234***			2.601***	1.411**		
	(1.033)	(1.150)			(0.876)	(0.709)		
SE								
ME			2.823**					
			(1.296)					
GE				0.341***				
				(0.153)				
Leffec	0.696**		−0.671*		−0.513**		0.900***	0.737***
	(0.327)		(0.354)		(0.252)		(0.283)	(0.281)
Tic	0.971**		0.839*	0.861***	1.151*			
	(0.673)		(0.711)	(0.676)	(0.642)			
Lage	0.263*	0.937**		1.661***				
	(1.551)	(1.883)		(1.493)				
Ltic	1.111*		2.751***					
	(0.650)		(0.782)					
sex_ma					1.809**			
					(0.811)			
stat_ma								
relig_ma			0.820**					
			(0.383)					
instruc_ma				0.838*			0.0410**	0.282***
				(0.433)			(0.277)	(0.285)
fortec_ma			1.107*	1.066*			1.937***	2.538***
			(0.649)	(0.582)			(0.751)	(0.798)
tranche_age			1.613**	0.962**				
			(0.794)	(0.698)				
Constant	3.475	3.272	−9.387	2.714	−0.907	−4.258**	−4.927**	−5.673***
	(3.640)	(4.324)	(873.6)	(3.598)	(1.516)	(1.716)	(2.026)	(2.187)
Observations	148	148	148	148	218	218	218	218

Standard errors in parentheses.
$^{*}p < 0.1$.
$^{**}p < 0.05$.
$^{***}p < 0.01$.

Table 12.
Multinomial logit model estimation of firms in the industrial sector.

Variables	Cameroon				Senegal			
	One form	Two forms	Three forms	Four forms	One form	Two forms	Three forms	Four forms
r_dev								
formality_ent		0.236***			1.468**	1.921***	0.989**	1.512**
		(0.151)			(0.671)	(0.593)	(0.769)	(0.633)
localisation	1.348	2.206**						
	(0.939)	(0.887)						
SE	1.904*	1.558*		2.254*		0.106***	0.649*	
	(1.067)	(0.903)		(1.200)		(0.511)	(0.623)	
ME	0.632**	2.060*		0.375*				
	(0.931)	(1.169)		(0.709)				
LE	−1.389**	−1.034*		−1.954***				
	(0.696)	(0.568)		(0.700)				
Leffec				0.763*			0.586**	0.775***
				(0.396)			(0.262)	(0.220)
Tic				0.0402*			0.317*	0.503**
				(0.585)			(0.845)	(0.597)
Lage		2.736**						
		(1.378)						
Ltic	0.852*						0.0447**	0.155***
	(0.510)						(0.324)	(0.301)
sex_ma	0.133**						0.0440***	0.912**
	(0.607)						(0.686)	(0.762)
stat_ma								
relig_ma	0.677**	0.227*	0.765**		0.466***	0.662*		
	(0.302)	(0.258)	(0.344)		(0.444)	(0.434)		
instruc_ma		0.496***	0.911**					
		(0.330)	(0.382)					
fortec_ma					0.0688*			
					(0.472)			
tranche_age		−1.234*						
		(0.681)						
Constant	−3.850	−8.431**	−20.05	−4.519	−1.599	−3.709**	−4.832**	−2.948*
	(3.412)	(3.320)	(1093)	(3.209)	(1.618)	(1.569)	(2.049)	(1.753)
Observations	190	190	190	190	281	281	281	281

Standard errors in parentheses.
$^{*}p < 0.1$.
$^{**}p < 0.05$.
$^{***}p < 0.01$.

Table 13.
Estimation of the multinomial logit model for trade firms.

Variables	Cameroon				Senegal			
	One form	Two forms	Three forms	Four forms	One form	Two forms	Three forms	Four forms
r_dev								3.069**
								(1.253)
formalite_ent		0. 086**	0.705***		3.495***	2.804***	4.933***	4.346***
		(0.621)	(0.327)		(0.833)	(0.777)	(1.044)	(1.011)
localisation	2.283**	1.189*	1.222*	2.037**	1.845***	1.667***	0.635***	0.511**
	(1.103)	(0.673)	(0.731)	(0.849)	(0.673)	(0.608)	(0.654)	(0.707)
PE	1.465*	0.196**	1.141*			1.020*		
	(0.776)	(0.798)	(0.684)			(0.578)		
ME		0.979**		0.232**				1.149**
		(0.658)		(0.784)				(0.988)
GE		0.109**		0.445**				0.735***
		(0.559)		(0.497)				(0.964)
Leffec			0.582**	0.593**	−0.656***			−0.491*
			(0.236)	(0.231)	(0.227)			(0.260)
Tic			0.0504***	0.116*				
			(0.496)	(0.502)				
Lage					0.436*	0.962***		
					(0.563)	(0.593)		
Ltic			0.207**		0.568*	0.510*	0.440***	0.156***
			(0.450)		(0.291)	(0.284)	(0.361)	(0.368)
sex_ma	0.586**	0.999**	0.650**	0.683*	0.435**	0.159***		0.510*
	(0.481)	(0.446)	(0.432)	(0.421)	(0.730)	(0.775)		(0.929)
stat_ma				0.450**				0.834**
				(0.189)				(0.363)
relig_ma								
instruc_ma		0.151**	0.105***	0.0387***		0.154**		0.248**
		(0.258)	(0.243)	(0.236)		(0.236)		(0.306)
fortec_ma			0.0653**	0.0987***	1.100**			1.913***
			(0.434)	(0.413)	(0.520)			(0.725)
tranche_age						−0.791*		
						(0.444)		
Constant	−6.267**	−3.089	−0.279	−2.953	−2.150	−4.382***	−18.34	−3.790*
	(2.988)	(2.537)	(2.463)	(2.485)	(1.649)	(1.683)	(547.7)	(1.978)
Observations	296	296	296	296	212	212	212	212

Standard errors in parentheses.
**p < 0.1.*
***p < 0.05.*
****p < 0.01.*

Table 14.
Estimation of the multinomial logit model for service firms.

Author details

Martin Ndzana* and Gregory Mvogo
Department of Decision Support and Information systems, Higher School of Economics and Business, University of Douala; and Agricultural Research, Innovation and Development Centre (CARID), Douala, Cameroon

*Address all correspondence to: ndzanajaures@gmail.com

References

[1] Statsenko L, Corral de Zubielqui G. Customer collaboration, service firms' diversification and innovation. Industrial Marketing Management. 2019;**85**(2020): 180-196. DOI: 10.1016/j.indmarman. 2019.09.013

[2] Wadho W, Azam C. Innovation and frm performance in developing countries: The case of Pakistani textile and apparel manufacturers. Research Policy. 2018;**47**(2018):1283-1294

[3] Zhang S, Yang D, Shumin Q, Bao X, Li J. Open Innovation and frm performance: Evidence from the Chinese mechanical manufacturing industry. Journal of Engineering and Technology Management. 2018;**48**(Apr–Jun):76-86. DOI: 10.1016/j.jengtecman.2018.04.004

[4] Martínez-Romero M, Martínez-Alonso R, Casado-Belmonte M, Diéguez-Soto J. Family management and firm performance: The interaction effect of technological innovation efficiency. In: Leitão NA, editor. Studies on Entrepreneurship, Structural Change and Industrial Dynamics. Cham: Springer; 2020. pp. 229-248

[5] OECD. Oslo Manual: Guidelines for Collecting and Interpreting Innovation Data. 3rd ed. Paris: OECD Publishing; 2005

[6] Edeh J, Obodoechi D, Ramos-Hidalgo E. Effects of innovation strategies on export performance: New empirical evidence from developing market firms. Technological Forecasting and Social Change. 2020;**158**(2020):120-167

[7] Lee R, Lee J-H, Garrett T. Synergy effects of innovation on frm performance. Journal of Business Research. 2019;**99**(2019):507-515. DOI: 10.1016/j.jbusres.2017.08.032

[8] Ndzana M, Onomo M, Mvogo G, Bedzeme T. Innovation and small and medium enterprises' performance in Cameroon. Journal of Small Business and Enterprise Development. 2021;**28**(5): 724-743. DOI: 10.1108/JSBED-06-2020-0188

[9] GEM. L'entreprenariat au Cameroun: Une forte volonté de créer des acteurs... des anbitions entrepreneuriales limitées...et un écosystème entrepreneurial à parfaire. trois_Rivières: Global Entrepreurship Monitor; 2017

[10] De Beer J, Armstrong C. Open innovation and knowledge appropriation in Africa micro and small enterprises (MSEs). The African Journal of Information and Communication. 2015; **2015**(16):60-71

[11] ILO. Enquête auprès des Entreprises Informelles du Cameroun. Genève: Bureau Internationale du Travail; 2017

[12] Hamelink M, Opdenakker R. How business model innovation affects firm performance in the energy storage market. Renewable Energy. 2018;**131** (February 2019):120-127. DOI: 10.1016/j. renene.2018.07.051

[13] La Porta R, Shleifer A. Informality and development. Journal of Economic Perspectives. 2014;**28**:109-123

[14] Camisón C, Villar-López A. Organizational innovation as an enabler of technological innovation capabilities and firm performance. Journal of Business Research. 2014;**67**:2891-2902

[15] Donbesuur F, Ampong G, Owusu-Yirenkyi D, Chu I. Technological innovation, organizational innovation and international performance of SMEs:

The moderating role of domestic institutional environment. Technological Forecasting and Social Change. 2020;**161** (2020):120-252

[16] Gunday G, Ulusoy G, Kilic K, Alpkan L. Effects of innovation types on firm performance. International Journal of Production and Economics. 2011;**133** (2011):662-676

[17] Latan H, Jabbour Chiappetta JC, Jabbour Loppes De Sousa AB, Fiorini PF. Innovative efforts of ISO 9001-certified manufacturing firms: Evidence of links between determinants of innovation, continuous innovation and firm performance. International Journal of Production Economics. 2019;**223**(May 2020):107526. DOI: 10.1016/j.ijpe.2019.107526

[18] Bigliardi B. The Effect of Innovation on Financial Performance: A Research Study Involving SMEs. Innovation: Management, Policy and Practice. 2013; **15**(2):245-255

[19] Rosenbusch N, Brinckmann J, Bausch A. Is innovation always beneficial? A meta-analysis of the relationship between innovation and performance in SMEs. Journal of Business Venturing. 2011;**26**(4):441-457

[20] Terziovski M. Innovation practice and its performance implications in small to medium enterprises (SMEs) in the manufacturing sector: A resource-based view. Strategic Management Journal. 2010;**31**(8): 892-902

[21] Van Auken H, Madrid-Guijarro A, Garcia_Perez-de-Lema D. Innovation and performance in Spanish manufacturing SMEs. International Journal of Entrepreneurship and Innovation Management. 2008;**8**(1): 36-56

[22] Goedhuys M, Janz N, Mohnen P. What drives productivity in tanzanian manufacturing Frms: Technology or business environment? European Journal of Development Research. 2008;**2**: 199-218

[23] Osei A, Yunfei S, Appienti W, Forkuoh S. Product innovation and SMEs performance in the manufacturing sector of Ghana. Journal of Economics, Management and Trade. 2016;**3**(15):1-14. DOI: 10.9734/BJEMT/2016/29906

[24] Beaman L, Magruder J, Robinson J. Minding small change among small firms in Kenya. Journal of Development Economics. 2014;**108**:69-86. DOI: 10.1016/j.jdeveco.2013.12.010

[25] Mendi P, Mudida R. The effect on innovation of beginning informal: Empirical evidence from Kenya. Technological Forecasting and Social Change. 2017;**131**(June 2018):326-335. DOI: 10.1016/j.techfore.2017.06.002

[26] Fu X, Mohnen P, Zanello G. Innovation and Productivity in Formal and Informal Frms in Ghana. Technological Forecasting and Social Change. 2018;**131**(2018):315-325

[27] Radicic D, Djalilov K. The impact of technological and non-technological innovations on export intensity in SMEs. Journal of Small Business and Enterprise Development. 2019;**26**(4):612-638. DOI: 10.1108/JSBED-08-2018-0259

[28] Avenyo KE, Konte M, Mohnen P. Product innovation and informal market competition in Sub-saharan Africa. Journal of Evolutionary Economics. 2020;**3**:1-33

[29] Mendi P, Costamagna R. Managing innovation under competitive pressure from informal producers. Technological Forecasting and Social Change. 2016;**114**

(January 2017):192-202. DOI: 10.1016/j.techfore.2016.08.013

[30] Heredia J, Flores A, Gesdes C, Heredia W. Effects of informal competition on innovation performance: The case of pacific alliance. Journal of Technology Management & Innovation. 2017;**12**(4):22-28

[31] McGahan A. Challenges of the informal economy for the field of management. Academic Management Perspective. 2012;**26**(3):12-21

[32] Li M, Wei J, Mckiernan P, Ng Cw D, Law K. Impacts of informal networks on innovation performance: Evidence in Shanghai. Chinese Management Studies. 2015;**1**:105-120

[33] George G, McGahan M, Prabhu J. Innovation for inclusive growth: Towards a theoretical framework and a research agenda. Journal of Management Studies. 2012;**49**(4):661-683

[34] von Hippel E. Democratizing Innovation Book Collections on Project MUSE. Cambridge, MA: MIT Press; 2005. p. 204

[35] Mollick E, Alicia R. Democratizing innovation and the capital access: The role of crowdfunding. California Management Review. 2016;**58**(2):72-87

[36] Links Mhula AL, Hart T, Jacobs P. The dynamics of local innovations among formal and informal enterprises: Stories from rural South Africa. African Journal of Science, Technology, Innovation and Development. 2014;**6**(3):175-184

[37] Wiliams CC, Kosta B. Evaluationg the impact of informal sector competitors on the performance of formal enterprises: Evidence from Bosnia and Herzegovina. Journal of Developmental Enterpreneurship. 2020; **25**(2):205-274

[38] Donkor J, Donkor G, Kankam-Kwarteng AE. Innovative capability, strategic goals and financial performance of SMEs in Ghana. Asia Pacific Journal of Innovation and Entrepreneurship. 2018; **12**(2):238-254

[39] Freel M-S, Robson P-A. Small firm innovation, growth and performance: Evidence from Scotland and Northern England. International Small Business Journal. 2004;**26**(6):561-575

[40] Orser B, Riding A. The influence of gender on the adoption of technology among SMEs. International Journal of Entrepreneurship and Small Bunisess. 2018;**33**(4):5-14

[41] Ramadani V, Hisrich R, Abazi-Alili H, Dana PP, Abazi-Bexheti. Product innovation and firm performance in transition economies: A multi-stage estimation approach. Technological Forecasting and Social Change. 2019;**140**(2019):271-280. DOI: 10.1016/j.techfore.2018.12.010

[42] Desjardins J. L'Analyse de la Régression Logistique. Tutorial in Quantitative Methods for Psychology. 2005;**1**(1):35-41

[43] Ayalew M, Xianzhi Z. The effect of financial constraints on innovation in developing countries: Evidence from 11 African countries. Asian Review of Accounting. 2019;**28**(3):273-308

[44] Nkakene M. Investissements immatériels et performance des PME camerounaises,. Rapport de recherche du FR-CIEA N°37/12; 2012

[45] Avenyo EK. Innovation and the performance of informal micro, small and medium-scaled enterprises

(MSMEs) in Ghana: A gender perspective. In: Paper presented at 4th AfricaLics International Conference. Dar es Salaam: Tanzania; 2019. pp. 1-36

[46] Akinwale OY, Adepoju OA, Olomu OM. The impact of technological innovation on SME's profitability in Nigeria. International Journal of Research, Innovation and Commercialisation. 2017;**1**(1):57-73

[47] Olaleye DF. The key determinants of innovation in small and medium scale enterprises in southwestern Nigeria. European Scientific Journal. 2015;**11**(13): 465-479

[48] Sakala Z, Kolster J. Innovation et productivité: analyse empirique pour les pays de l'Afrique du Nord. Notes économiques de la BAD. Abidjan, Côte d'Ivoire: African Development Bank; 2014

[49] Abdu M, Jibir A. Determinants of firms innovation in Nigeria. Kasetsart Journal of Social Sciences. 2018;**39**(3): 448-456

[50] Agwu AG, Agbanike T, Uwajumogu N, Ogbuagu RA. How do firms combine different types of innovation? A multivariate probit approach. African Journal of Science, Technology, Innovation and Development. 2020;**12** (2):173-185

[51] ILO. Diagnostic de l'économie informelle au Sénégal. Genève: Bureau international du Travail; 2020

Chapter 3

The Influence of Foreign Investors on the Development of Polish Enterprises: A Case Study of Bank Polska Kasa Opieki Spółka Akcyjna

Waldemar Milewicz

Abstract

Pursuant to the definition proposed by Eurostat, foreign direct investment takes place when a resident entity in one economy seeks to obtain a lasting interest in an enterprise resident in another economy. A lasting interest implies the existence of a long-term relationship between the direct investor and the enterprise, and an investor's significant influence on the management of the enterprise. Foreign investors do not only exert impact on a given company's board of directors but, importantly, provide production capital in privatized companies. Additionally, they equip them with both know-how on the performed economic activity and technical know-how. They send their specialists, who introduce international standards in daughter companies smoothly. In this paper, the author deals with the impact of a foreign investor on the development of Bank Pekao. A literature review is applied for this aim. It covers a detailed analysis of transaction documentation and post-audit statements of the Supreme Audit Office and delegations of the Ministry of State Treasury. Thanks to research, it can be assessed how UniCredito Italiano has positively influenced the operation of Polish bank after the acquisition of shares. Thereby, the results of this study contest popular opinion about exploitation of domestic employees by foreign companies.

Keywords: foreign direct investment, know-how, performance

1. Introduction

From the methodological point of view, there are many definitions of foreign direct investment. The subject of this article leads to a special emphasis on definitions which refer to the creation of a long-term relationship between an investor and the company in which the shares are acquired [1]. According to the IMF definition, direct investment reflects the aim of obtaining a lasting interest by a resident entity of one economy (direct investor) in an enterprise that is resident in another economy (the direct investment enterprise). The "lasting interest" implies the existence of a long-term relationship between the direct investor and the direct investment enterprise and a significant degree of influence on the management [2] of the latter. Direct investment involves both the initial transaction establishing the relationship between the investor and the enterprise and all subsequent capital transactions between them and among affiliated enterprises, both incorporated and unincorporated [3]. The similar dimension gives the definition proposed by the Organization for Economic Cooperation and Development (OECD). Due to its interpretation, foreign direct investment means investment that aims at causing long-lasting relationships. In turn, the latter reflects an interest of an economic entity of one country in an economic entity of a country other than the country of permanent residency of the direct investor [4].

In Polish conditions, private economic entities did not have sufficient savings to acquire shares in state enterprises at appropriate prices. The state does not have the possibility to maximize profit with only domestic investors [5]. For this reason, it seems advantageous from the financial point of view to expand the investment circle to include foreign investors (or privatization with the help of foreign investors only) [6]. Moreover, the rapid incorporation of foreign, especially international, enterprises into the national economy compensates for the lack of competitiveness of national entities [7, 8]. The reason for this is a lack of know-how, outdated technology and inadequate product quality. Companies with foreign shareholding usually have a high share of equity, use modern technology [9] and pay above-average salaries [10].

On the basis of the investment data of foreign companies, it can be concluded that they carry out restructuring faster and more intensively than comparable companies with a purely domestic shareholding [11]. This can lead to higher unemployment in the short term [12]. In the long term [13], however, the development of the acquired company will be more evenly matched by subsequent investments [14]. The role of foreign investors in privatized companies refers to providing not only production capital but, above all, business know-how and technical know-how. Both types of knowledge can be passed on by foreign specialists, who should eliminate the previously insufficient level of efficiency [15] and parallelly smoothly introduce international standards in new subsidiaries [16]. Due to a specific "dissemination" of imported know-how, the effect of improved efficiency also influences domestic companies that have not yet been privatized [17].

At this point, it is worth showing how the issue of the impact of foreign investors on domestic firms is presented by other scholars (**Table 1**).

The above-mentioned positive aspects of foreign investors' activity in Poland were accompanied by relevant changes in the law. The Act on Companies with Foreign Participation played an important role here. It came into force on June 4, 1991. The following legal regulations were enshrined in the law:

- the creation of a general obligation to obtain a permit to set up a company (the exceptions were ports, airports, real estate trade, part of the arms industry, wholesale trade in imported consumer goods, legal services)
- free transfer of profits and capital
- transfer of the total amount remaining after the sale or liquidation of the company
- liquidation of the minimum amount at foreign initial capital
- liquidation of permission to acquire shares in privatized Polish enterprises

Author	Article	Abstract
Abdul Majeed, Ping Jiang, Mahmood Ahmad, Muhammad Asif Khan, Judit Olah	The Impact of Foreign Direct Investment on Financial Development: New Evidence from Panel Cointegration and Causality Analysis	The aim of this paper is to analyze the relationship between foreign direct investments and financial development in Bahrain. The estimation of financial development effects was performed for the period 1978 to 2015, which covers the political conflicts that happened in Middle East area (Arab Spring).
Made Gitanadya Aryani, Annisa Pratamasari	The Relationship between Foreign Direct Investment Influx, Economic Growth, and Financial Institutions in ASEAN-6	The object of this research is ASEAN members, because Southeast Asia is a dynamically growing region in terms of economy; hence, it attracts FDI influx. ASEAN is also a challenging object in terms of the degree of variability in financial market among its members.
Manpreet Kaur, Surendra S. Yadav, Vinayshil Gautam	Financial System Development and Foreign Direct Investment: A Panel Data Study for BRIC Countries	The article analyzes the impact of financial system development on FDI with respect to BRIC countries for the period 1991 to 2010. Using the panel data analyses, fixed and random effect, our results conclude that FDI inflows to BRIC countries are influenced by banking sector and stock market variables, used as a proxy for financial development.
Luca Papi	Foreign Direct Investment in the Banking Sector: A Transitional Economy Perspective	In this paper, we use new statistics on Foreign Direct Investment (FDI) in Transitional Economies (TEs) to analyze the issue of foreign ownership in the banking sector, examining the implications for the host banking sector. After considering the potential benefits and risks associated with foreign investment in the banking sector, and on the basis of some empirical results, we reach the conclusion that FDI provides valuable opportunities for the development of the host banking sector.
Hameed Khan, Umair Khan	Financial development and FDI inflows in China	In this paper, the authors revisit the nexus of financial development and FDI inflows, in Chinese perspective, incorporating the vital role of institutional quality and other important variables in this paradigm. Using ARDL bound testing and VECM procedures, they establish causality by exploiting variations in financial development and FDI.
Ritika Sharma	FDI in Indian banking sector	The present study aims at providing detailed information about FDI inflows in India during the subsequent years. The analysis is fully based on secondary data collected through different websites and journals. The project aims at providing information of present FDI policy, year-wise FDI inflows, advantages and disadvantages of FDI, RBI policy, foreign portfolio investment, impact and importance of FDI in banking sector, etc.
Laura Alfaro, Jasmina Chauvin	Foreign Direct Investment, Finance, and Economic Development	Research has sought to understand how foreign direct investment affects host economies. This paper reviews the empirical literature, specifically addressing the question: How does FDI affect economic development of host countries, and what is the role of local financial markets in mediating the potential benefits?

Source: [18–23].

Table 1.
The impact of foreign investors on domestic enterprises—A review of exemplary research articles.

- equal status of foreign companies and parent companies (tax exemptions for investments over EUR 2 million, liquidation of the turnover tax)

- taking over the accounting standards applicable in the European Union [24]

This liberalization of the conditions for foreign entities in terms of acquiring Polish companies resulted in rapid capital inflow to Poland. In this paper, the author presents the positive side of privatization in his home country. He deals with the impact of a foreign investor on the development of Bank Pekao S.A. A literature review is applied for this aim. It covers detailed analysis of transaction documentation and post-audit statements of both the Supreme Audit Office and delegations of the Ministry of State Treasury. Thanks to research, it can be assessed how UniCredito Italiano has positively influenced the operation of Pekao S.A. after the acquisition of shares. The objective of this analysis is to show, on the basis of these documents, what changes have taken place in the bank following the entry of a strategic investor. Furthermore, the author shows, on the basis of precise figures, what financial support there was from the new shareholder. It is also important in this context that it is not only about showing the material impact but also about presenting the contributed know-how, e.g. in the form of trainings. Thereby, the results of this study contest popular opinion about exploitation of domestic employees by foreign companies. Furthermore, novelty of my research lies in detailed description of ownership changes in banking with regard to its impact on certain companies and, thereby, the development of capital market in Poland.

2. Agreement between the state Treasury of the Republic of Poland and UniCredito Italiano S.p.a. and Allianz AG.: Sale of shares of Pekao S.A.

Privatization of Bank Pekao S.A. took place in the form of public offering – State Treasury sold 52.1% of shares in Bank Polska Kasa Opieki Spółka Akcyjna. The buyer was a consortium of entities: Credit Suisse First Boston, UniCredito Italiano S.p.A. and Allianz AG. It prepared an investment plan. It undertook to guarantee a capital increase of PLN 1000 million over a two-year period. Investors, in turn, assumed that Pekao would invest PLN 2000 million over five years. In the final offer for the purchase of shares, the consortium indicated that it fully appreciated the importance of Pekao for the Polish economy. For this reason, it intended to develop Pekao into a modern financial institution. According to purchase agreement, it was supposed to:

- financially support infrastructure development,

- financially support the development of small and medium enterprises, as well as large companies,

- participate in creating the market for Treasury debt securities,

- support Polish exports.

The partners of the consortium considered the privatization of Pekao as a unique opportunity to create a leader in Poland. He was to be able to face the challenges of Poland's membership in the European Union. In addition, his task was to create a strong base for development in the broader regional context of Central Europe [25].

3. New distribution network in the bank

In the area of retail banking, the investor's goal was to transform Pekao into the largest provider of financial services for the population in Poland. This was achieved by maintaining and further penetrating the existing customer base. Penetration, in turn, took place by "bringing" the bank closer to customers and expanding the customer base (through selective expansion of the bank's geographical coverage). In accordance with that, Pekao has rapidly developed the branch network in Silesia, Poznań, Gdańsk (the bank had a limited presence there) and strengthened its presence in Warsaw. This process was accompanied by events that also affected the qualitative development of the bank and, thus, the capital market in Poland:

- transfer of employees from the so-called back office (administration) to sales and customer contact (so-called front office); this process was supported by IT systems and incentive programs;
- increasing the range of branch networks; this was done by carrying out further transformation – from large universal branches into small specialized branches;
- development of distribution range and level of services (mobile sales teams were introduced and permanent distribution channels were supplemented with automated channels, i.e. ATMs, telephone service, etc.);
- improving the coverage of the distribution network (as for individual customers).

In the field of business services, specifically in the field of business financing, Pekao had a leading market share at the time. The consortium successfully strengthened this position. This was due to the support of Pekao's financing of infrastructure projects, e.g. in the energy sector, telecommunications and construction of toll motorways. The consortium, in addition, strengthened the position of Bank Pekao as a market leader by:

- building the so-called network of account managers,
- introducing a customer contact management system,
- making greater use of distribution networks,
- improving the position in handling foreign transactions,
- facilitating access to funds from the European Union.

As a result, the improvement of the distribution network closely linked to the regrouping of employees in the company significantly strengthened Pekao's position in the banking market. Thanks to that, Pekao bank developed in terms of quality, which in turn contributed to the qualitative development of capital market in Poland.

4. Product support in the bank

In the field of services for small and medium enterprises, their development was very important from the point of view of maintaining strong economic growth in

Poland. Bearing this in mind, the strategic investor sought to strengthen Pekao's position in the small and medium-sized enterprise market. In this way, it influenced the qualitative development of the capital market in Poland. This was done by:

- further improvement of product quality (introduction of products with the features of the best products on the market; in addition, systematic combination of new products with ROR, e.g. mortgage development, credit cards, asset management and insurance),
- introduction of standard product packages (especially prepared for this category of medium-sized enterprises),
- simplification of credit processes (in order to reduce service time without compromising the quality of the loan portfolio).

The qualitative impact on the Polish bank and on the Polish capital market on the part of the Uni Credit consortium was also reflected in another fact. According to the Italian bank's declaration, it passed its knowledge about developing and managing banking products in the following areas, among others:

- credit cards with revolving credit;
- consumer loans (in the field of valuation methodology and credibility assessment system – so-called scoring system);
- products related to asset management (trust funds, portfolio management and financial planning techniques),
- cash flow management (so-called cash management),
- electronic banking products,
- project financing.

Knowledge in the field of credit, asset management, cash management, electronic banking and project financing has enriched Bank Pekao with new know-how and, thus, has made a significant qualitative contribution to its development and the capital market in Poland.

In addition, in terms of asset management and bancassurance, a consortium of investors has contributed to the professional implementation of the bancassurance concept at Pekao. This created additional revenue for Pekao. The consortium's activities in this area strengthened the position of Bank Pekao towards customers. This was also done by introducing the offer of a full range of financial services (so-called one-stop shopping, financial supermarket approach). The above activities of the strategic investor made a significant qualitative contribution to the development of Bank Pekao, the banking system in Poland, and thus the Polish capital market.

The consortium's intentions in the area of bancassurance were also made more concrete in the fact that branches and mobile teams of advisers-sales representatives of Bank Pekao were used to sell insurance products and banking products (e.g. mortgage loans, car loans). Bank Pekao has also used Allianz's operations in Poland.

It used the existing products of the German insurer to create its own insurance business from scratch. It happened without the need to involve capital and human resources. To sum up, the consortium of investors, by developing bancassurance activities at Bank Pekao, significantly supported the qualitative development of Bank Pekao, the banking market, and thus the capital market in Poland.

In addition, the UniCredit consortium provided Pekao with a range of Polish and international investment funds for use in its distribution network. It is worth noting that at the level of people's wealth then in the country, it was not expected that this would be a significant strengthening of the bank's revenues. Despite this, owning such products has strengthened Pekao's image as a universal financial institution. It also meant readiness to take advantage of the growing popularity of these products. Thanks to the strategic investor's involvement in investment funds, the bank's brokerage activities were further strengthened. Obviously, this translated into the qualitative development of Pekao bank, the banking system, and, thus, the capital market in Poland.

The consortium introduced portfolio management techniques at Pekao bank with a fixed risk/return relationship. It based its activity on the position of the leader of the Central Brokerage House Pekao in brokerage activities. As a result, it increased the quality of services offered at Pekao Bank and reduced their cost. An important element of the qualitative impact on Bank Pekao was also the fact that the consortium had unique qualifications that were needed to implement these activities. It resulted from experience in creating and introducing products and sales methods. The above activities of the Uni Credit consortium improved the position of Bank Pekao on the banking market and made a significant qualitative contribution to the development of the Polish capital market.

The qualitative impact of the UniCredit-Allianz consortium in the field of bancassurance on Bank Pekao was conditioned by the fact that the entities UniCredit and Allianz were partners in the field of bancassurance in Italy. UniCredit sold life and property policies. It did this through a network of over 2000 branches. Unicredit also had an important position in asset management (it managed over EUR 60 million). It was one of the leading brokerage houses in Italy. In turn, Allianz was the world leader in insurance – it concluded a bancassurance agreement with partners in 12 countries. The above facts meant that UniCredit brought significant know-how to Bank Pekao, supported its qualitative development, and, thus, contributed to the development of the capital market in Poland.

The guarantee of a positive qualitative impact on the part of UniCredit on the Polish capital market was additionally the fact that it is one of the leading banks in Italy. In fact, it transferred know-how from its home market to the Polish market. As a result, Bank Pekao received knowledge from the Italian investor in the field of business services. In addition, thanks to Italian financial institution, 500 account managers started servicing companies. The strategic investor also used modern systems to manage contacts with Pekao clients. Not without significance in this context was the fact that UniCredit's credit processes (guarantee methods and so-called early warning systems) corresponded to the latest developments in this field on a global scale. They were considered exemplary in the Italian banking system. Thanks to this, the impact of know-how on the part of UniCredit on Bank Pekao and the Polish banking system and, thus, the capital market in terms of quality was significantly positive.

5. New management methods in the bank

UniCredit declared that it could support Pekao in introducing new IT systems. The Italian bank had experience in transferring systems to other banks. Evidence of this was, for example, the completion by the subsidiary UniCredit (dealing in IT) of the integration of Banca CRT, Banca Cariveron and Cassamarca in 2000. It did so by adding 1000 branches to a common IT platform. Similarly, the implementation of the new IT system – one of the most important processes at Bank Pekao – has been successfully completed. It happened, thanks to the knowledge and experience of specialists from UniCredito Italiano delegated to Polish bank. In addition, UniCredito Italiano has taken actions in the area of credit, market and operational risk management at Bank Pekao. They were oriented towards improving the degree of integration of Pekao's policy with the overall operations of the UniCredito Italiano group. They were also successful. Therefore, it is justified to state that UniCredito Italiano, through its activities in the Pekao bank in the area of IT system and risk, has strengthened its qualitative position. In this way, it made a qualitative contribution to the development of the capital market in Poland.

UniCredit also provided support for Pekao in other areas:

- creation and management of customer service centers, so-called call center;
- establishment of branches (UniCredit had extensive knowledge in the field of branch restructuring and in the introduction of new types of branches);
- marketing using databases (UniCredit was a precursor in supporting sales using databases);
- creating and managing sales teams, specializing of sales teams (UniCredit has introduced sales methods tailored to specific customer segments);
- sales team management (UniCredit has developed knowledge in improving the efficiency of its sales teams; this was done by introducing individual incentive systems based on financial goals);
- credit risk management (UniCredit has introduced modern credit procedures, credit application assessments and behavioral assessment systems),
- Management Information System, so-called MIS (UniCredit has introduced a modern MIS system at the individual customer and group level),
- motivation of the management, investment banking (UniCredit provided its knowledge in the field of analysis, reaching certain level of turnover, marketing and risk management; this complemented Pekao skills),
- operating activities (Pekao's systems and its operating environment lagged far behind the best international standards; thanks to UniCredit, Bank Pekao reached global standards; this means that it skipped the trial-and-error stage that Western banks, including UniCredit, had to pass in the eighties).
- introducing organizational changes, so-called change management (merger of banks is a huge task; it includes remodeling of responsibilities, retraining and, as a last resort, dismissal; UniCredit had vast experience in this field – it was the effect of merging seven banks).

The impact of the above factors on the quality position of Bank Pekao was considerable. It remained in connection with the qualitative development of the Polish capital market.

6. New programs in the company aimed at development of employees

Regarding the social program, the consortium introduced a number of activities at Bank Pekao. They were aimed at improving the education and motivation of employees. It was about incentive pay, management exchange program and training. UniCredit, while caring for the intellectual development of Pekao bank employees, also made a significant qualitative contribution to its development. Thus, it contributed to the qualitative development of a capital market in Poland.

The needs of the Pekao employees on the part of the UniCredit consortium were also secured, thanks to:

- pension fund introduced,
- stocks program for management and employees,
- health care,
- scholarships.

The above elements, brought in by a strategic investor, also had a significant impact on the qualitative development of Pekao bank, and thus the capital market in Poland.

In accordance with the Pekao program for local communities, UniCredit supported higher education in Poland. This was due to the fact that the strategic investor has close links with the Universita Commerciale Luigi Boccioni (the most prestigious and recognized economic university in Italy). In addition, UniCredit also supported the commercial activities of the Pekao bank (with the use of database constructed on the basis of the customer portfolio). The activity of a strategic investor in the educational and operational field at Bank Pekao has made a qualitative contribution to the development of Bank Pekao, and thus – the capital market in Poland.

7. Consortium's investment obligations

The UniCredit consortium has fulfilled its commitment that Pekao's capitalization should be sufficient to implement its development plans. At the same time, it helped maintain the capital adequacy ratio of Pekao at a certain level. It was recognized by international financial markets as safe for a bank from the Central Europe region. The UniCredit consortium, by helping to implement Pekao's plans and maintaining the required level of solvency ratio, has contributed to the qualitative development of Pekao, and thus the capital market in Poland.

The Guaranteed Investment Program should also be mentioned as an important element of the qualitative impact on the development of the Polish capital market in the aspect of UniCredit offer. Under this program, the UniCredit consortium was to invest at least PLN 1 billion in Pekao over a three-year period. In addition, the consortium prepared an investment plan. It assumed that the bank would invest PLN 2 billion over a five-year period.

As for the implementation of individual strategic investor's obligations, it was presented in the "Information on the implementation of non-price obligations" [26]. It shows that:

- the consortium made a commitment to Pekao; at the General Meeting of Shareholders of the bank undertook to vote for the allocation of the bank's profits to share capital, supplementary capital or reserve capitals; in this way, it was to contribute to the qualitative development of capital market in Poland; by voting for the allocation of profits to share capital, the consortium strengthened the bank's quality position; according to the report of Ernst and Young Audit Sp. z o.o. of June 30, 2003, the performance of this obligation was confirmed in 1998, 1999 and 2000; thus, it was decided that there were no grounds for charging contractual penalties; thereby UniCredit made a contribution to the qualitative development of the capital market in Poland

- during the guaranteed investment period, UniCredit was to retain 50.09% of the share capital of Pekao Bank, and Allianz – 2% plus 25,000 shares; in addition, they were not to conclude any agreement obliging to sell Pekao bank shares; according to the report of Ernst and Young Audit Sp. z o.o. of June 30, 2003, the performance of the undertaking was confirmed; additional statements of the Ministry of Treasury were also a document confirming the performance of the undertaking (Application); thus, it should be stated that UniCredit has made a qualitative contribution to the development of the capital market in Poland; by not selling Pekao bank shares, it strengthened the bank's quality position and contributed to its development

- the investor has made a commitment regarding the management of Bank Pekao's assets; according to it, it was not to cause the bank to be liquidated or dissolved (until the end of the guaranteed investment period); additional statements of the Ministry of Treasury were also a document confirming the performance of the commitment (Application); in conclusion, it should be stated that UniCredit has made a qualitative contribution to the development of the capital market in Poland; without liquidating Pekao, it strengthened the bank's quality position and contributed to its development

- as regards the management of Bank Pekao's assets, the investor was also not to cause the bank to sell all or part of its assets (until the end of the guaranteed investment period); additional statements of the Ministry of Treasury were also a document confirming the fulfillment of this obligation (Application); in conclusion, it should be stated that UniCredit has made a qualitative contribution to the development of the capital market in Poland; by not selling Pekao's assets, it strengthened the bank's quality position and contributed to its development.

The UniCredit investor also undertook that within a period of five years from the signing of the contract, it will support the development of Pekao. This process was to be in line with the provisions of the Bank's Development Program and take place by:

- investing in development programs,
- strengthening the bank's position on the market,
- improving access to information technology, know-how and organizational methods,
- providing licenses and other rights and solutions necessary to implement the Bank's Development Program.

According to the report of Ernst and Young Audit Sp. z o.o. of June 30, 2003, it was found that the above obligations were met and there were no grounds for charging contractual penalties. The document confirming their implementation was also the investor's annual report for 2000 and additional speeches by the Ministry of Treasury (Application); UniCredit made a qualitative contribution to the development of the capital market in Poland. By investing in development programs and improving access to information technologies, know-how and organizational methods at Pekao Bank, it strengthened its quality position and contributed to its development.

The investor also undertook to fully support Pekao's strategy. It consisted of developing and consolidating his position. It was to be the leading universal bank in Poland and a leading financial institution in Central and Eastern Europe. Other important commitments were that UniCredit:

a. undertook to give Pekao the status of UniCredit's main investment in Central Europe;

b. was to give Pekao a right of priority in connection with all purchase transactions (they were made by UniCredit in the republics of the former USSR, as well as in the Czech Republic and Slovakia, with the exception of investments in Polno Banka S.A.);

c. was to support Pekao's strategic plans for expanding into other countries;

d. was to make joint decisions with Pekao regarding transactions carried out in Romania and Bulgaria (in the event that UniCredit indicated a potential investment, the bank was to have pre-emptive rights over such investment).

All the above liabilities, according to the report of Ernst and Young Audit Sp. z o.o. of June 30, 2003, were carried out in a timely manner. In this way, the strategic investor strengthened the quality position of Pekao Bank and thus contributed to the qualitative development of the capital market in Poland.

At that time, the main goal of the bank and the UniCredito Italiano group was to increase the value for the shareholders of Bank Pekao. The strategic investor did this by maintaining and strengthening the leading position of Bank Pekao in selected areas of activity:

- retail banking with an emphasis on investment funds,
- mortgages,
- credit cards,

- support for microenterprises.

This goal was achieved, thanks to the implemented improvements from the UniCredit group. It introduced in the Pekao bank such elements as product innovation, modern distribution channels and a comprehensive customer service model (a combination of VIP customer service and small and medium-sized enterprises). UniCredit has dynamically developed more advanced distribution channels, such as online banking, telephone banking and direct sales. All the elements listed above, implemented in the Pekao bank by a strategic investor, strengthened its quality position. In this way, UniCredit has contributed to the qualitative development of the capital market in Poland.

In accordance with art. 3 par 12 paragraph 2 sales contracts, the strategic investor undertook to provide technical, technological and organizational solutions to Pekao. Therefore, UniCredit initiated a comprehensive restructuring process of the Pekao bank. It began after the investor purchased the majority stake.

In art. 4 par 2 of the sales contract, the investor assumed that Pekao bank, thanks to the support of UniCredit, will make investments in the amount of PLN 1000 million (Guaranteed Investments). This was in accordance with Annex 11 of the contract. The auditor found that the commitment had been carried out. The UniCredito Italiano consortium stated that in the period up to August 2002, its capital expenditure at Pekao bank amounted to PLN 1010.8 million. In addition, by the end of 2002, he allocated PLN 140 million for investments at Pekao Bank.

Capital expenditures were also subordinated to Pekao's development strategy. They were related to the development of Pekao's business. This was done through its subsidiaries and affiliates. During the Guaranteed Investments period, the bank developed its activities as planned (to the extent provided in Annex 9 to the contract). Thanks to the aforementioned significant capital and investment outlays, UniCredito Italiano has strengthened the quality position of Pekao. Thus, it contributed to the qualitative development of the capital market in Poland.

In art. 4 par 2 of sales contracts, the UniCredito consortium undertook to acquire shares in Bank Pekao for a total amount of PLN 1 billion. This was specified in the contract as a guaranteed capital increase. As a result of the guaranteed capital increase, the capital of Bank Pekao increased by PLN 1000.1 million. Thanks to the increase in capital by UniCredito Italiano, Bank Pekao strengthened its quality position. The increase in the amount of capital gave the bank extensive investment opportunities. Thus, UniCredito Italiano has contributed to the qualitative development of the capital market in Poland [27].

8. Conclusions

In fact, UniCredit (according to source documents) provided Pekao with considerable knowledge and experience at the strategic and operational levels. The innovative activities of the strategic investor were also particularly important here[1]. This manifested itself, for example, in the fact that permanent distribution channels were supplemented with automated channels (i.e. ATMs, telephone service). Moreover, the

[1] At this point, it should be mentioned that those who study innovative activities in banking should, in future, pay more attention to all digitization processes, which are currently progressing at a dizzying pace in the banking sector.

Italian investor introduced products with the features of the best products on the market and combined new products with mortgage development, credit cards, asset management and insurance. Similarly, the implementation of the new IT system, which stood for innovative support of Pekao's operational activity, has been successfully completed. It happened, thanks to the knowledge and experience of specialists from UniCredito Italiano delegated to Polish financial institution. In this way, Italian bank made a significant contribution to the qualitative development of Bank Pekao, and thus the Polish capital market. Thus, according to Gustav Dieckheuer's theory (see: Introduction), it compensated for the lack of outdated technology and inadequate product quality. By sharing knowledge and experience in these areas, the strategic investor strengthened the quality position of the bank. Evidence of the possibilities for a positive impact of the Italian bank was its growth and profitability. It also had experience in integrating different banks into the group. As a result of the partnership with the Pekao consortium, it strengthened its leadership position in Polish banking. Thanks to this, the quality of the bank's products and services has also improved, and its international prestige has increased. This was reflected in the qualitative development of the bank and, thus, of the capital market in Poland. At the same time, the strategic investor maintained Pekao's identity so outside – through its brand and image – and internally in Poland.

The investor consortium reviewed Pekao's activities and trends on the Polish market. It did so by having a clear and properly implemented Pekao development plan. In this way, the consortium of investors assisted Pekao's management board in facing the competition. At the same time, it reversed the erosion of market share and strengthened the bank's operational efficiency. The following areas have been strengthened:

- retail banking,
- service for small and medium enterprises,
- asset management,
- bancassurance,
- business services,
- investment banking,
- international activities,
- operational efficiency.

The above actions of the strategic investor have made a significant qualitative contribution to the development of the bank and, thus, to the development of the capital market in Poland. By strengthening individual areas at Bank Pekao, the Uni Credit consortium has significantly improved the bank's quality position on the market.

Classifications

JEL Classifications: F21, L33

Author details

Waldemar Milewicz
German Economy Research Unit, World Economy Institute, Warsaw School of Economics Building A, Rakowiecka, Warsaw

*Address all correspondence to: wmilew@sgh.waw.pl

References

[1] Available from: https://ec.europa.eu/eurostat/statistics-explained/index.php/Glossary:Foreign_direct_investment_(FDI)

[2] Przybylska K. Zagraniczne inwestycje bezpośrednie jako podstawowa forma ekspansji gospodarczej transnarodowych korporacji (Foreign direct investment as the basic form of economic expansion of transnational corporations). Vol. 585. Kraków: Published by Zeszyty Naukowe Akademii Ekonomicznej w Krakowie; 2001. p. 12

[3] Duce, M. 2003. Definitions of Foreign Direct Investment (FDI): A methodological note, BIS Meeting of the CGFS Working Group on FDI in the financial sector (31.07.2003)

[4] Organisation for Economic Co-operation and Development. OECD Benchmark Definition of Foreign Direct Investment. Fourth ed. Paris: OECD Publishing; 2008. p. 48

[5] Bradburd R. Privatization of Natural Monopoly Public Enterprises: The Regulation Issue. New York: Published by Review of Industrial Organization; 1992. p. 38. DOI: 10.1007/BF01027074

[6] Massmann E. Alternative Privatisierungsstrategien in MOE-Staaten: eine Analyse unterschiedlicher Verfahren im Hinblick auf ihre Anwendung am Beispiel der Republik Polen (Alternative privatization strategies in CEE countries: an analysis of different procedures with regard to their application using the example of the Republic of Poland). Köln: Published by Josef Eul Verlag; 2002

[7] Karaszewski W. Bezpośrednie inwestycje zagraniczne. Polska na tle świata. (Foreign Direct Investment. Poland against the background of the world). Toruń: Published by Dom Organizatora; 2004. p. 19

[8] Táncošová J. The role of foreign direct investment in the economy of Slovakia. Entrepreneurship and Sustainability Issues. 2019;**6**(4):2127-2135. DOI: 10.9770/jesi.2019.6.4(40)

[9] Lederer V. Zur Transformation mittel- und osteuropäischer Betriebe: ein Vergleich ostdeutscher, polnischer und bulgarischer Betriebe auf qualitativ-empirischer Grundlage (On the transformation of Central and Eastern European enterprises: A comparison of East German, Polish and Bulgarian companies on a qualitative-empirical basis). München und Mering: Published by Rainer Hampp Verlag; 1998. p. 57

[10] Cohen D. How Privatization Increases Inequality. Oakland: Published by In the Public Interest; 2016. p. 4

[11] Goodman JB, Loveman GW. Does Privatization Serve the Public Interest? Boston: Harvard Business Review; 1991

[12] Fabuš M, Csabay M. State aid and investment: Case of Slovakia. Entrepreneurship and Sustainability Issues. 2018;**6**(2):480-488. DOI: 10.9770/jesi.2018.6.2(1)

[13] Marques-dos-Santos JE. The Long-Run Fiscal Impact of Privatisation: An Empirical Assessment of the Brazilian Experience. 2007. p. 2. Available from: https://pdfs.semanticscholar.org/6d6c/02656e443ececc6d2917a86dc358001d5db3.pdf

[14] Zeibote Z, Volkova T, Todorov K. The impact of globalization on regional

development and competitiveness: cases of selected regions. Insights into Regional Development. 2019;**1**(1):33-47. DOI: 10.9770/ird.2019.1.1(3)

[15] Pettinger, T. 2017. Advantages and problems of privatisation. Available from: https://www.economicshelp.org/blog/501/economics/advantages-of-privatisation/

[16] McCulloch R. New perspectives on foreign direct investment. In: Froot KA, editor. Foreign Direct Investment. Chicago: Published by University of Chicago Press; 1993. pp. 43-45

[17] Dieckheuer G. 1990. Die Bedeutung ausländischer Direktinvestitionen fűr Beschäftigung, Struktur, Wettbewerbsfähigkeit und Wachstum von Volkswirtschaften – dargestellt am Beispiel der Bundesrepublik Deutschland 1950-1990. Volkswirtschaftliche Diskussionsbeiträge, no. 131. (The importance of foreign direct investment for employment, structure, competitiveness and growth of economies - illustrated by the example of the Federal Republic of Germany 1950-1990. Economic Discussion Contributions, no. 131.) Münster: Published by Westfälische Wilhelms-Universität Münster, p. 19

[18] Available from: https://www.academia.edu/8296960/FDI_in_Indian_banking_sector

[19] Available from: https://www.cjournal.cz/files/397.pdf

[20] Available from: http://www.economics-ejournal.org/dataset/PDFs/discussionpapers_2019-54.pdf

[21] Available from: https://econpapers.repec.org/article/saeglobus/v_3a14_3ay_3a2013_3ai_3a4_3ap_3a729-742.htm

[22] Available from: https://papers.ssrn.com/sol3/papers.cfm?abstract_id=2908440

[23] Available from: https://www.scitepress.org/Papers/2018/102726/102726.pdf, https://econpapers.repec.org/paper/csldevewp/133.htm

[24] Poznańska K. Transformationsprozesse in Polen. Hamburg: Published by Verlag Dr. Kovaĉ; 1994. pp. 63-67

[25] Final offer for the purchase of Polska Kasa Opieki S.A. shares, submitted by Credit Suisse First Boston, UniCredito Italiano S.p.A. and Allianz AG, 5 March 1999, p. 4

[26] Information on the implementation of non-price obligations arising from the Share Purchase Agreement of Bank Polska Kasa Opieki S.A., concluded on June 23, 1999 between the State Treasury of the Republic of Poland, represented by the Minister of the Treasury and UniCredito Italiano S.p.A. and Allianz Aktiengesellschaft, p. 3.

[27] Application by the Ministry of the Treasury for information on the implementation of the commitment of 3.08.2000, 9.02.2001, 27.12.2001, 19.11.2002; Answers given to UniCredito Italiano of September 21, 2000, in which performance of the undertaking was found in 1999, of April 13, 2001, in which the performance of the undertaking was found in 2000, of February 12, 2002, in which the performance of the undertaking was found in 2001, of January 9, 2003, in which performance of the undertaking was confirmed in 2002

Chapter 4

Innovation and Entrepreneurial Ecosystems

Alina Ianioglo

Abstract

Nowadays special attention is paid to ecosystem conditions that encourage innovation and entrepreneurship. This chapter provides a critical review and expands the understanding of the concepts of the innovation ecosystem and entrepreneurial ecosystem. The entrepreneurial ecosystem represents a collection of actors that interact within a geographically bound entrepreneurial environment and factors, which contribute to the development of productive entrepreneurship. Innovation ecosystems represent communities of interacting actors that support innovation processes and create technologies and innovations. The focus of the innovation ecosystem is on value creation through the creation of innovations, while the focus of the entrepreneurship ecosystem is on the development of entrepreneurship. There are differences between the two concepts, but also the relationships and interactions, which are revealed in the chapter. Also, there are highlighted the framework, components and features of both entrepreneurial and innovation ecosystems.

Keywords: system, entrepreneurship, entrepreneurial ecosystem, innovation, innovation ecosystem, networks, knowledge

1. Introduction

In current conditions of tough competition, technological advances, digitalization and exponential growth of knowledge, special attention is devoted to entrepreneurship and innovation. Entrepreneurship and innovation are considered the drivers of competitiveness, social and economic development.

Entrepreneurship is essential in amplifying innovation, creating jobs, satisfying customer demands and other economic impacts. It is well known that an important trait of entrepreneurs is their ability to innovate. Globally, people are searching innovative ways to capitalise on an idea, start a new venture and develop the business. At the same time, innovation is recognised as an important factor in fostering growth. In the attempt to improve the efficiency of operation with scarce resources, enterprises do not function in isolation but undertake entrepreneurial activity within a community of interdependent actors. The process of commercialising an idea encompasses numerous parties, and the creation of entrepreneurial and innovation ecosystems has been considered to be an effective way to nurture and support this process [1].

Innovation and entrepreneurial ecosystems are recent phenomenon phenomena that have attracted the increasing attention of policymakers, business practitioners and academics. Today, the ecosystem conditions that encourage entrepreneurial innovations and high-potential entrepreneurship became of great importance [2].

Nevertheless, according to J. Schumpeter, entrepreneurship and innovation have been strongly related [3], the innovation ecosystem and entrepreneurial ecosystem literature mainly evolve in parallel [4]. Nevertheless, there are a number of studies that discuss the main types of ecosystems, the literature suffers from a lack of development. There is little research that has considered the interactions between innovation and entrepreneurial ecosystems.

This chapter provides a critical review and expands the understanding of the concepts of the innovation ecosystem and entrepreneurial ecosystem, their commonalities and differences.

2. Introducing the concept of ecosystem

The term ecosystem (ecological system) has been adapted from biology, where it is seen as a community of living organisms interacting with various components of their environment [5]. Thus, the 'eco' is related to the environment and the 'system' implies a set of interrelated parts that operate as a unit.

J. Moore [6] translated the ecosystem metaphor into the management field. He drew a parallel between a biological system and business, stating that like organisms in nature, companies interact with each other and exist in a given business environment. Since then, the ecosystem literature has obtained increased popularity in academia, business, management and policy. In the last decades, different research streams have been developed: business ecosystem [6], followed by the innovation ecosystem, the entrepreneurial ecosystem, the knowledge ecosystem and others. These ecosystems mainly differ depending on the types of actors involved and the nature of the value proposition.

In business and management, the concept of an 'ecosystem' describes "collectives of heterogeneous, yet complementary organisations" who jointly generate an ecosystem-level output, thus extending beyond the outputs and activities of any individual participant of the ecosystem [7].

There are four commonalities that distinguish ecosystems from other organisational collectives: the system-level outcome, participant heterogeneity, nature of interdependence among ecosystem participants and coordination mechanisms [8]. The presence of one of them does not distinguish an ecosystem, but the combination of all four characteristics is unique to ecosystems. The system approach does not explain the relationship between stakeholders. Comparing to the concept of system, which is perceived as static, the ecosystem concept should not be perceived from a linear point of view, it has a dynamic perspective. Entrepreneurship is a complex process and every ecosystem comprises a unique set of actors and interactions, which determine its evolution and shape the present and future state of the ecosystem.

3. Entrepreneurial ecosystem

The entrepreneurial ecosystem concept consists of two aspects: ecosystem described earlier, and entrepreneurial. Entrepreneurial refers to the process of entrepreneurship. The latter is defined as "the process of creating value by bringing together a unique combination of resources to exploit an opportunity" [9].

Entrepreneurial ecosystems have evolved as a result of the changing debates about entrepreneurship. In exploring entrepreneurship, the studies shifted the focus from the personality approach to the broader social and economic environment, where enterprises are located. Entrepreneurial ecosystems offer a more realistic representation of entrepreneurial activity.

E.J. Malecki states that entrepreneurial ecosystem emerged in the early 1990s, identifying contributions from Moore's 'business ecosystem', Van de Ven's 'infrastructure for entrepreneurship' and Spilling's concept of a local 'entrepreneurial system' [10].

Some of the most influential studies, which have driven the popularity of the concept of the entrepreneurial ecosystem are publications of D. Isenberg [11], B. Feld [12], C. Mason and R. Brown [13], E. Stam [14], B. Spigel [15] and others, highlighting that the community and culture in a specific place can have a significant impact on entrepreneurship process. The components of the ecosystem and local context can influence the choices, entrepreneurs make and decisions they take.

The ecological aspect of the entrepreneurial ecosystem has links to 'economic gardening', an entrepreneurial approach to local economic development [13]. Entrepreneurial ecosystems should create supportive environments that foster both new business start-ups and high-growth firms. Thus, there should be created a environment that promotes the creation of new ventures, including innovative start-ups, as well as the development of enterprises. Some practitioners view predominantly start-ups within entrepreneurial ecosystems, but ecosystems are not just about start-ups, the role of larger enterprises should not be diminished.

The entrepreneurial ecosystem is a recent notion with various definitions suggested, but there is not a widely shared definition yet. B. Spigel [15] sees the concept as a conceptual umbrella that comprises different perspectives on the geography of entrepreneurship rather than a coherent theory.

A list of main definitions of entrepreneurial ecosystem provided in the literature is presented in **Table 1**. Some definitions consider the role of the components (e.g. [13, 14]), while others emphasise the interaction among the elements (e.g. [4]).

The analysis of the main definitions allowed identifying main *characteristics of entrepreneurial ecosystem*:

- there are various actors and factors involved;
- interactions, interdependent relationships between different actors are essential in an ecosystem;
- the focus is on growth-oriented entrepreneurship;
- dynamic and systemic nature of the concept;
- there should be an element of spatiality/locality.

The entrepreneurial ecosystem implies a shift from traditional economic thinking focused mainly on companies and markets towards new thinking about people and networks. In all presented and other definitions, entrepreneurship does not occur in

Authors	Definition	Features
Isenberg, 2010	entrepreneurship ecosystem "consists of a set of individual elements—such as leadership, culture, capital markets, and open-minded customers—that combine in complex ways" [11].	The focus is on components of the ecosystem.
Acs et al., 2014	"dynamic, institutionally embedded interaction between entrepreneurial attitudes, ability, and aspirations, by individuals, which drives the allocation of resources through the creation and operation of new ventures" [4].	Emphasis the allocation of resources as an outcome, and dynamic nature of the ecosystem.
Mason & Brown, 2014	entrepreneurial ecosystem is "a set of interconnected entrepreneurial actors (...), entrepreneurial organisations (...), institutions (...) and entrepreneurial processes (....) which formally and informally coalesce to connect, mediate and govern the performance within the local entrepreneurial environment" [13].	The definition is quite comprehensive, nevertheless without specifying ecosystem outcomes.
Stam, 2015	entrepreneurial ecosystem is "a set of interdependent actors and factors coordinated in such a way that they enable productive entrepreneurship" [14].	Highlights productive entrepreneurship as the output of the ecosystem.
Mack & Mayer, 2016	entrepreneurial ecosystems "consist of interacting components, which foster new firm formation and associated regional entrepreneurial activities" [16].	Focus mainly on new ventures and regional aspect.
Audretsch & Belitski, 2017	entrepreneurial ecosystems defined as "institutional and organisational as well as other systemic factors that interact and influence identification and commercialisation of entrepreneurial opportunities" [17].	Emphasis the system-level context.
Bruns et al., 2017	entrepreneurial ecosystem represents a "multidimensional set of interacting factors that moderate the effect of entrepreneurial activity on economic growth" [18].	Highlights the role of interacting factors in entrepreneurial activity.
Spigel, 2017	entrepreneurial ecosystems are "combinations of social, political, economic, and cultural elements within a region that support the development and growth of innovative startups and encourage nascent entrepreneurs and other actors to take the risks of starting, funding, and otherwise assisting high-risk ventures" [15].	Emphasis the governance and the spatial constraint of the ecosystem, focusing on start-ups and high-risk ventures.
Spigel et al., 2020	entrepreneurial ecosystems defined as the "regional collection of actors (such as entrepreneurs, advisors, mentors, and workers) and factors (cultural outlooks, policies, R&D systems, and networks) that all contribute to the creation and survival of high-growth ventures" [19].	The definition involves a regional aspect and focuses on high-growth ventures.
Van Rijnsoever, 2020	entrepreneurial ecosystem is seen as "a set of actors that interact and exchange resources in a network under an institutional regime and an infrastructure" [20].	Implies a specific institutional regime and infrastructure.

Source: own elaboration.

Table 1.
Some of the main definitions of the entrepreneurial ecosystem.

isolation, at the centre of the entrepreneurial ecosystem are the actors with all their interactions and relationships. These relationships among actors support entrepreneurial activities.

Within the concept of the entrepreneurial ecosystem, many authors mainly consider the creation and activity of high-growth start-ups and scale-ups. E. Stam [14] introduced the concept of productive entrepreneurship, which is interpreted as an entrepreneurial activity that "creates aggregate welfare increases", it is seen as an "outcome of successful ambitious entrepreneurship". Ambitious entrepreneurs are those entrepreneurs who seek to get a higher performance of their ventures and to quickly scale-up [21]. Generally, the modern literature emphasis growth-oriented entrepreneurship. The ecosystem supports venture development and contributes to the determination of opportunities for collaboration and competition. A rich entrepreneurial ecosystem fosters entrepreneurship and therefore value creation, contributing to social and economic development.

A sustainable ecosystem cannot be instantly implemented, it takes decades of effort to achieve this. It should be noted that many studies have been focused on a static picture of entrepreneurial ecosystems. The dynamic perspective started to be considered recently in the literature. Entrepreneurial ecosystems are evolving through the interactions between actors. Also, the dynamics depend on factors of national and international order, as well as cultural specificities in a given locality. Thus, the entrepreneurial ecosystem represents a complex system, which evolves over time.

Entrepreneurial ecosystems have a spatial dimension. Generally, they are geographically bounded, but there is no limitation regarding their geographic scale. The ecosystem emerges through successful interaction between the actors at different levels: university campuses, cities, regional and national levels [22]. Also, there might be links between different ecosystems [23].

Generally, we can conclude that an *entrepreneurial ecosystem* represents a collection of actors that interact within a geographically bound entrepreneurial environment and factors, which contribute to the development of productive entrepreneurship.

The entrepreneurial ecosystem is a complex system that focuses on entrepreneurship and facilitates venture development, leading to value creation in the community.

There is no universal model of an entrepreneurial ecosystem. The structure of entrepreneurial ecosystems is unique, it may vary in different geographic communities, but what is important is their ability to ensure systems-based support for entrepreneurial activity, enabling access to markets, finance, human and intellectual capital.

The dynamic and systemic nature of the entrepreneurial ecosystem involves various actors, institutions and processes.

There are specific components of the entrepreneurial ecosystem, which are necessary to sustain entrepreneurship in a given territory. Several models of the entrepreneurial ecosystem were suggested, for example, the model by D. Isenberg [11]; G. Foster et al. [24], P. Vogel [25]; E. Stam [26], T. Mazzarol [27], B. Spigel [15].

D. Isenberg identified six domains within the entrepreneurial system: a conducive culture, enabling policies and leadership, availability of appropriate finance, quality human capital, venture-friendly markets for products, and a range of institutional supports [28]. This model contains a totally 12 core components.

In comparison, the model suggested by J. Leendertsea, M. Schrijvers and E. Stam [29] emphasises causal relations and includes institutional arrangements (formal institutions, culture and networks of entrepreneurs), resource endowment elements (psychical infrastructure, demand, support services/ intermediaries, talent, knowledge, leadership and finance), outputs (productive entrepreneurship – an "entrepreneurial activity that creates aggregate welfare" [14]) and outcomes (value creation and economic growth). Besides the fact that the model reflects the importance of different actors and their interactions within the entrepreneurial ecosystem, it also reveals how these conditions support the entrepreneurial activities and value creation, which over time feedback into the system conditions.

Presented models reflect the components of a successful entrepreneurial ecosystem. At the same time, it is important to understand how these ecosystems evolve over time. An example of evolutionary dynamics of entrepreneurial ecosystems was developed by E. Mack and H. Mayer [16], which contain phases of birth, growth, sustainment and decline (self-renewal).

Therefore, there are different approaches to identify components of the entrepreneurial ecosystem, main approaches are presented in **Table 2**.

We can conclude that there are essential components that overlap or are similar, specifically: culture, markets, infrastructure, government, etc. The entrepreneurial ecosystem components are mutually interdependent and co-evolved.

Further, we will consider the main components that are crucial for a successful entrepreneurial ecosystem. We elaborate on the model suggested by E. Stam [14] and complement it with two more relevant components: education and training, innovation (**Figure 1**).

Even though there are more *components* to consider, we will focus on the main ones:

Infrastructure. Entrepreneurs are dependent on physical infrastructure, transportation, energy, telecommunications and others.

Markets/demand. Accessible markets (local, global) are essential to any enterprise. Customers with their needs create opportunities for entrepreneurship.

Human capital. It is an important component in the entrepreneurial ecosystem. Accessible skilled labour is a driver of success in the modern knowledge economy. Workers should have skills, abilities and expertise that meet the specific demand of enterprises.

Education and training. It is mainly provided by higher educational institutions. Universities disseminate and commercialise the knowledge; they represent the main resource for talent and are significant in an ecosystem.

Finance. Along with human capital, of great importance is the access to finance. Both are necessary and traditional and alternative sources of finance: microloans, bank loans, business angels, seed investors, venture capital, fintech, etc.

Networks. The networks of entrepreneurs provide an information flow, enabling an effective distribution of knowledge, labour and capital [30].

Policy and governance. Entrepreneurship depends on a context that is shaped by governments. The policies may encourage or hinder entrepreneurs. Efficient policies facilitate the development of the ecosystem. Additionally, there should be paid attention to the political context.

Support services. It includes a range of different organisations, intermediaries that provide support to businesses, for example, professional services (legal, accounting, insurance, consulting, technical experts), associations, mentors, clusters, business incubators, etc.

Culture: It represents the attitudes towards entrepreneurship. The culture and the presence of success stories can motivate or discourage entrepreneurial activities.

Knowledge. It refers to theoretical foundations, tacit, specialised, formal/informal knowledge that are used and generated.

Innovation. This is one of the main forces in entrepreneurial activity and allows exploiting opportunities.

DOI: http://dx.doi.org/10.5772/intechopen.102344

D. Isenberg [28]		G. Foster [24]	P. Vogel [25]	E. Stam [26]	T. Mazzarol [27]	B. Spigel [15]
Human capital	Labor	Human capital/ Workforce	Entrepreneurial actors	Talent	Human capital and workforce	Worker talent
	Educational institutions	Major universities as catalysts	Entrepreneurial education		Universities as catalysts	Universities
Markets	Networks		Networks	Networks		Networks
	Early customers	Accessible markets	Markets	Demand	Local and global markets	Open markets
Finance	Financial capital	Funding and finance	Financing	Finance	Funding and finance	Investment capital
Culture	Societal norms	Cultural Support	Culture	Culture	Culture	Supportive culture
	Success stories					Histories of entrepreneurship
Policy	Leadership			Leadership		
	Government	Regulatory framework & infrastructure	Government & regulations	Formal institutions	Government policy	Policy and governance
Supports	Infrastructure		Infrastructure	Physical infrastructure	Regulatory framework & infrastructure	Physical infrastructure
	Support professions	Support system	Startup support	Support services, intermedia-ries	Mentors, advisors and support systems	Support services
	Non-governm institutions					mentors and role models
		Education & training			Education & training	
			Innovation			
			Geographic location			
			Visibility			
				New knowledge		

Source: own elaboration.

Table 2.
Synthesis of the main approaches to identify components of entrepreneurial ecosystem.

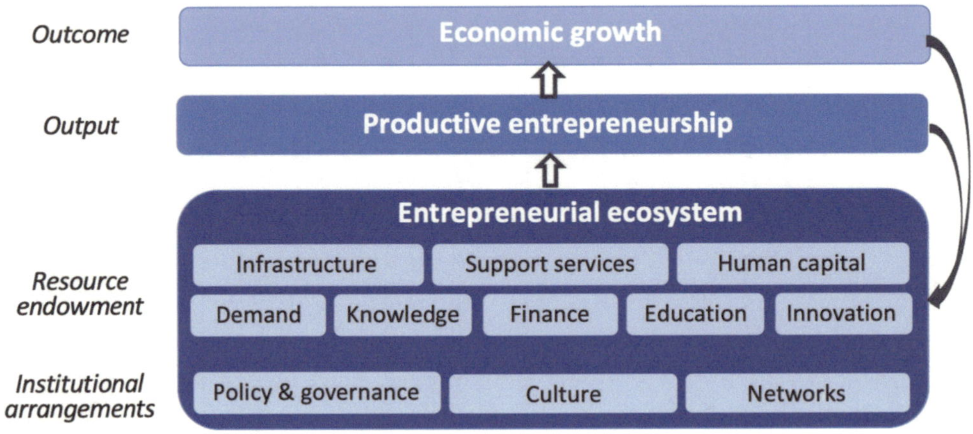

Figure 1.
Key elements, outputs and outcomes of the entrepreneurial ecosystem. Source: adapted from ref. [29].

Main *actors* in an entrepreneurial ecosystem are entrepreneurs, public sector, service providers (marketing, legal, etc.), financial institutions, academia, investors, non-government organisations, media, etc.

At the same time, it should be kept in mind, that there is no one key factor of success. There are multiple components, which vary in the different entrepreneurial ecosystem, each ecosystem will have its unique structure.

4. Innovation ecosystem

Literature on the innovation ecosystem, similar to the other concepts of the ecosystem in management, experienced significant growth in recent years. Predecessors of the innovation ecosystem are considered the innovation system and the business ecosystem.

Before defining the innovation ecosystem, we will take a look at the innovation aspect of the concept. According to Tidd et al., innovation is "a process of turning opportunity into new ideas and of putting these into widely used practice" [31]. Another definition states that innovation represents "the implementation of a new or significantly improved product (good or service), or process, a new marketing method, or a new organisational method in business practices, workplace organisation or external relations" [32]. At the same time, the concept 'new' could mean new to the world, new to a nation, new to a firm, etc.

The concept of innovation ecosystem became more widely used after the publication of a Harvard Business Review article by R. Adner. He defined an innovation ecosystem as "the collaborative arrangements through which firms combine their individual offerings into a coherent, customer-facing solution" [33]. Some definitions of the innovation ecosystem are presented in **Table 3**.

A more recent and quite comprehensive definition was provided by O. Granstrand, and M. Holgersson: an innovation ecosystem is "the evolving set of actors, activities, and artifacts, and the institutions and relations, including complementary and substitute relations, that are important for the innovative performance of an actor or a population of actors" [37].

This definition highlights five components: actors, activities, relations (collaborative, competitive), artefacts (products and services, tangible and intangible resources, technological and non-technological resources, and other types of system inputs and outputs, including innovations) and evolution.

Authors	Definition
R. Adner, 2006	innovation ecosystems are "the collaborative arrangements through which firms combine their individual offerings into a coherent, customer-facing solution" [33].
D. Jackson, 2011	defines an innovation ecosystem as the "complex relationships that are formed between actors or entities whose functional goal is to enable technology development and innovation" [34].
S.Nambisan & R. Baron, 2013	innovation ecosystems refer to "a loosely interconnected network of companies and other entities that coevolve capabilities around a shared set of technologies, knowledge, or skills, and work cooperatively and competitively to develop new products and services" [35].
E. Autio, 2021	an innovation ecosystem is "a community of hierarchically independent, yet interdependent heterogeneous participants who collectively generate a coherent, ecosystem-level output and related value offering targeted at a defined user audience" [36].
O. Granstrand, & M. Holgersson, 2020	an innovation ecosystem is "the evolving set of actors, activities, and artefacts, and the institutions and relations, including complementary and substitute relations, that are important for the innovative performance of an actor or a population of actors" [37].

Source: own elaboration.

Table 3.
Some of the main definitions of innovation ecosystem.

Innovation has evolved beyond the boundaries of single companies towards a more network-based approach [38]. This is because innovations are implemented through a system with complex networks, where organisations interact with each other to foster innovation.

While innovation systems can be governed by public policies, being static concepts, innovation ecosystems are perceived as self-organised, dynamic structures, which evolve along with changing market conditions. Similar to an entrepreneurial ecosystem, a successful innovation ecosystem is the result of a long process of evolution and may have different stages of maturity.

Due to the involvement in the network, each ecosystem participant is symbiotic to and co-evolves with other participants [39]. Fast changes in the business environment and increasing uncertainty determine organisations both to compete and to cooperate in order to achieve success. All actors in an innovation ecosystem contribute to the co-creation of the value of a whole ecosystem, which would be hardly possible to produce by a single firm.

Differing from innovation systems, innovation ecosystems involve collaborative activities in the innovation process. In an ecosystem, information, knowledge and tangible resources move around the network. Technology is the main resource of innovation, at the same time, not every technology leads to innovation. In order an idea to become an innovation, it should be implemented. In a successful innovation ecosystem, innovation outputs are commercialised. Therefore, the innovation ecosystem encompasses both R&D and commercial areas.

Ecosystems represent networks of organisations that combine efforts to produce and implement innovations. Ecosystems "'do' something to create value for someone" [36]. In contrast to business ecosystems, which focus on value capture, innovation ecosystems focus on value creation [40].

Some important*features of innovation ecosystem* are:

- an innovation ecosystem is dynamic and flexible;
- is characterised by complex relationships between actors;
- interdependence between actors;
- openness;
- network effect;
- co-evolution;
- co-creation of value in the ecosystem.

The innovation ecosystem model is related to various spatial levels, ranging from company, city, regional, to national and even global levels. Ecosystems have also been considered at non-spatial levels of analysis, meaning that the focal firm and its complementors and suppliers are not necessarily located in the same region, as long as they belong to the same sector [7].

Innovation ecosystem consists of interacting actors, relationships, resources and conditions that either enable or impede innovation (**Figure 2**).

Main *actors* in the innovation ecosystem are: entrepreneurs, government, academia (both educational and R&D institutions), industry (various associations), supporting institutions (institutions that provide specialised, professional assistance), financial system (e.g. financial institutions, investors, business angels, venture capitalists) and civil society (non-government organisations, media, etc.) [41]. Innovation ecosystem includes the following main *elements*: human capital,

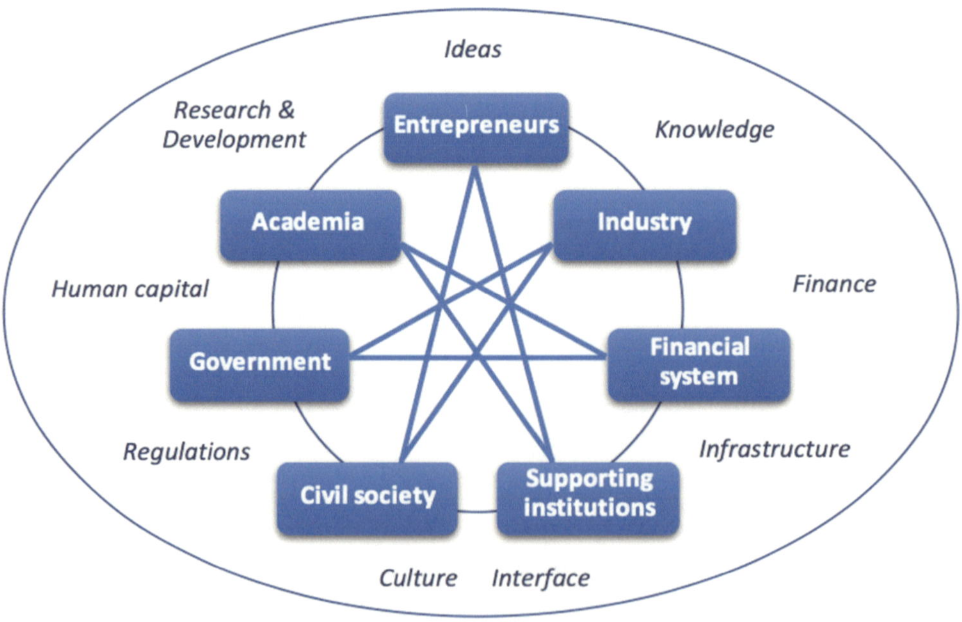

Figure 2.
Innovation ecosystem. Source: own elaboration.

knowledge, infrastructure, regulations, ideas, finance, research and development, the interface between actors, culture.

Therefore, innovation ecosystems represent communities of interacting actors that support innovation processes and create technologies and innovations. By using the infrastructure and resources, better ways of doing things are developed and implemented.

5. Similarities and differences between innovation ecosystem and entrepreneurial ecosystem

The concept of ecosystem became widely used in the field of innovation and entrepreneurship by academics, policymakers and practitioners. The entrepreneurial and innovation ecosystems evolved to understand why some places grow, while others stagnate and therefore to explain successful socio-economic development in a particular geographical area. They share closely related issues and have many similarities, being at the same time different in various aspects.

Ensuring growth depends on the social and economic environment for innovation and entrepreneurship. Entrepreneurial and innovation ecosystems represent complex systems with the following common features: self-organisation, complex components, interdependent relationships between different actors, non-linearity, i.e. dynamic nature, adaptability. Both concepts have their roots in the ecosystemic foundation, thus are characterised by non-linearity and include a multitude of actors and factors, interacting at many levels. In an ecosystem, a key feature is that firms do not just compete with each other using their own resources, but cooperate, interact and use shared resources, knowledge, networks, infrastructure and support to co-create value. Both ecosystems encompass collaboration between new, small ventures and large organisations. Also, innovation is considered to be central to innovation ecosystems as well as entrepreneurial ecosystems. Innovation represents one of the main motive forces of entrepreneurial ecosystems [42].

However, there are a number of differences between the analysed concept, particularly in the units of analysis used, context mechanisms, roles of individual agents in regional economic development [43].

Although there is some relation between the concepts of entrepreneurship and innovation, it should be mentioned that not all entrepreneurs innovate, as well as not all innovations are about entrepreneurial opportunities [44].

In general, both analysed ecosystems involve similar actors, the difference is in the role they play in the respective ecosystem. In terms of the components, there are some components that are essential for both ecosystems, for example, human resources, finance, infrastructure, governance, etc. At the same time each ecosystem includes a number of components that are mainly characteristic to them, for example, ideas, research and development to the innovation ecosystem, and visibility, innovation, markets to entrepreneurial ecosystems (**Figure 3**).

Innovation ecosystem represents a network of legally independent economic agents of different line-ups who can be direct competitors, but collaborate to create a comprehensive value proposition for customers. On the other hand, in an entrepreneurial ecosystem, there is no value offering targeted at a defined audience. Instead, it implies a network of interrelated economic agents from a specific area and results in the creation of new ventures and stimulation of regional development [45]. The proximity of all actors is essential in an entrepreneurial ecosystem, which is place-based,

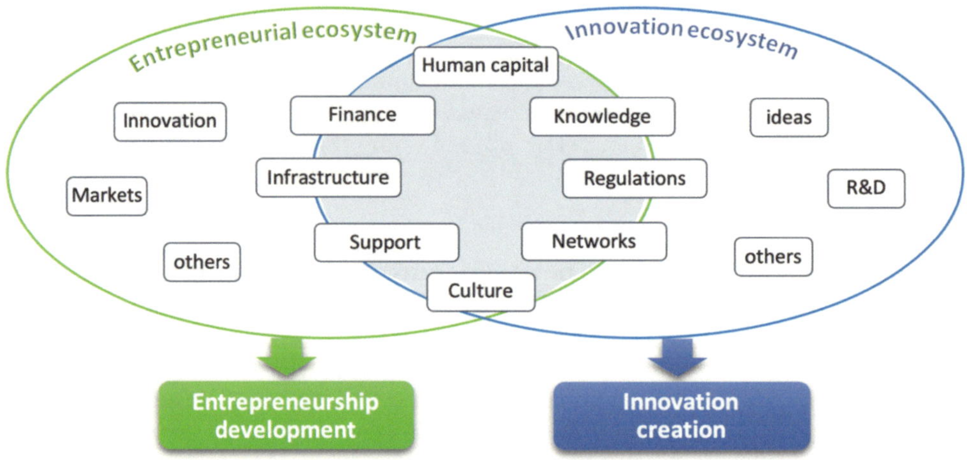

Figure 3.
Entrepreneurial ecosystem vs. innovation ecosystem. Source: own elaboration.

but it is more flexible in an innovation ecosystem, which is non-location specific with a possible virtual presence.

Another difference between innovation ecosystem and entrepreneurial ecosystem refers to various emphases: it is on innovation and entrepreneurs correspondingly. Innovation ecosystems focus on value creation through innovation creation, while entrepreneurial ecosystems focus on entrepreneurship development. Entrepreneurial activity, as an output of the entrepreneurial ecosystem, creates opportunities for innovation. While innovation, in turn, contributes to new value creation, which is the outcome of an entrepreneurial ecosystem [21]. The output of collaboration in the innovation ecosystem may be in form of various innovations, innovative technologies, products, services, it supports processes of innovation. The output of the entrepreneurial ecosystem is the entrepreneurial activity and entrepreneurship development, where the interactions between actors and the infrastructure create conditions for new ventures creation.

6. Conclusions

The chapter expanded the understanding of the concepts of the entrepreneurial ecosystem and innovation ecosystem. Different approaches to defining entrepreneurial and innovation ecosystems, as well as determining their structures were considered.

Innovation and entrepreneurial ecosystems are a recent phenomenon that evolved in an attempt to determine what leads to the success of socio-economic development.

An entrepreneurial ecosystem represents a collection of actors that interact within a geographically bound entrepreneurial environment and factors, which contribute to the development of productive entrepreneurship.

On the other hand, innovation ecosystems represent communities of interacting actors that support innovation processes and create technologies and innovations.

It was identified that entrepreneurial and innovation ecosystems are complex systems with the following common features: self-organisation; encompass complex components; interdependent relationships between different actors; non-linearity, i.e. dynamic nature; adaptability. Innovation is considered to be central to both innovation and entrepreneurial ecosystems, innovation ecosystems representing an important context for entrepreneurship. However, there are a number of differences between the entrepreneurial and innovation ecosystems, particularly in location, the main focus, context mechanisms, roles of individual actors, the output of the ecosystem. Both analysed ecosystems involve mainly similar actors, the difference is in the role they play in the respective ecosystem. It was stated that innovation ecosystems focus on value creation through the development of innovations, while entrepreneurial ecosystems on entrepreneurship development.

Nevertheless, further research is needed to identify the direction of strengthening entrepreneurial and innovation ecosystems, which will contribute to economic growth and social development.

Author details

Alina Ianioglo
National Institute for Economic Research, Chisinau, Republic of Moldova

*Address all correspondence to: alina.ianioglo@gmail.com

References

[1] Xu Z, Maas G. Innovation and entrepreneurial ecosystems as important building blocks. In: Maas G, Jones P, editors. Transformational Entrepreneurship Practices. Cham: Palgrave Pivot; 2019. pp. 15-32. DOI: 10.1007/978-3-030-11524-1_2

[2] Guerrero M, Martínez-Chávez M. Aligning regional and business strategies: Looking inside the Basque Country entrepreneurial innovation ecosystem. Thunderbird International Business Review. 2020;**2020**(62):607-621. DOI: 10.1002/tie.22162

[3] Schumpeter J. The Theory of Economic Development: An Inquiry into Profits, Capital, Credit, Interest, and the Business Cycle. Cambridge, MA: Harvard University Press; 1934

[4] Acs ZJ, Autio E, Szerb L. National systems of entrepreneurship: Measurement issues and policy implications. Research Policy. 2014; **43**(3):476-494. DOI: 10.1016/j.respol. 2013.08.016

[5] Tansley AG. The use and abuse of vegetational concepts and terms. Ecology. 1935;**16**(3):284-307

[6] Moore JF. Predators and prey: A new ecology of competition. Harvard Business Review. 1993;**71**(3):75-86

[7] Thomas LDW, Autio E. Innovation Ecosystems in Management: An Organizing Typology. In: Oxford Research Encyclopaedia of Business and Management. Oxford: Oxford University Press; 2020

[8] Autio E, Thomas LDW. Researching ecosystems in innovation contexts. Innovation & Management Review. 2021:1-14. DOI: 10.1108/ INMR-08-2021-0151

[9] Stevenson HH, Jarillo Mossi JC. Preserving entrepreneurship as companies grow. Journal of Business Strategy. 1986;**7**(1):10-23

[10] Malecki EJ. Entrepreneurship and entrepreneurial ecosystems. Geography Compass. 2018;**12**:e12359. DOI: 10.1111/ gec3.12359

[11] Isenberg DJ. How to start an entrepreneurial revolution. Harvard Business Review. 2010;**88**(6):40-50

[12] Feld B. Startup Communities: Building an Entrepreneurial Ecosystem in your City. New York: Wiley; 2012

[13] Mason C, Brown R. Entrepreneurial Ecosystems and Growth Oriented Entrepreneurship. Paris: Final Report to OECD; 2014. http://lib.davender. com/wp-content/uploads/2015/03/ Entrepreneurial-ecosystems-OECD.pdf

[14] Stam E. Entrepreneurial ecosystems and regional policy: A sympathetic critique. European Planning Studies. 2015;**23**(9):1759-1769. DOI: 10.1080/09654313.2015.1061484

[15] Spigel B. The relational organization of entrepreneurial ecosystems. Entrepreneurship Theory and Practice. 2017;**41**(1):49-72. DOI: 10.1111/ etap.12167

[16] Mack E, Mayer H. The evolutionary dynamics of entrepreneurial ecosystems. Urban Studies. 2016;**53**(10):2118-2133. DOI: 10.1177/0042098015586547

[17] Audretsch DB, Belitski M. Entrepreneurial ecosystems in cities:

Establishing the framework conditions. Journal of Technology Transfer. 2017;**42**(5):1030-1051. DOI: 10.1007/s10961-016-9473-8 Available at https://centaur.reading.ac.uk/61156/

[18] Bruns K, Bosma N, Sanders M, et al. Searching for the existence of entrepreneurial ecosystems: A regional cross-section growth regression approach. Small Business Economics. 2017;**49**:31-54. DOI: 10.1007/s11187-017-9866-6

[19] Spigel B, Kitagawa F, Mason C. A manifesto for researching entrepreneurial ecosystems. Local Economy. 2020;**35**(5):482-495. DOI: 10.1177/0269094220959052

[20] Van Rijnsoever FJ. Meeting, mating, and intermediating: How incubators can overcome weak network problems in entrepreneurial ecosystems. Research Policy. 2020;**49**:103884. DOI: 10.1016/j.respol.2019.103884

[21] Spigel B, Stam E. Entrepreneurial ecosystems. In: Blackburn R, De Clercq D & Heinonen J (eds). SAGE Handbook of Entrepreneurship and Small Business. London: 21, SAGE; 2018. DOI: 10.4135/9781473984080.n21

[22] Fredin S, Liden A. Entrepreneurial ecosystems: Towards a systemic approach to entrepreneurship? Geografisk Tidsskrift-Danish Journal of Geography. 2020;**120**(2):87-97. DOI: 10.1080/00167223.2020.1769491

[23] Wurth B, Stam E, Spigel B. Toward an entrepreneurial ecosystem research program. Entrepreneurship Theory and Practice. March 2021:1-50. DOI: 10.1177/1042258721998948

[24] Foster G, Shimizu C, Ciesinsik S, et al. Entrepreneurial Ecosystems around the World and Company Growth Dynamics, Industry Agenda. Geneva, Switzerland: World Economic Forum; 2013

[25] Vogel P. The employment outlook for youth: Building entrepreneurship ecosystems as a way forward. In: Conference Proceedings of the G20 Youth Forum. St. Petersburg, Russia: G20 Youth Forum; 2013. pp. 443-449

[26] Stam E. The Dutch Entrepreneurial Ecosystem. Utrecht: Birch Research; 2014. pp. 1-41. DOI: 10.2139/ssrn.2473475

[27] Mazzarol T. Growing and sustaining entrepreneurial ecosystems: What they are and the role of government policy. In: White Paper WP01-2014. Australia: Small Enterprise Association of Australia and New Zealand (SEAANZ); 2014

[28] Isenberg D. The entrepreneurship ecosystem strategy as a new paradigm for economic policy: Principles for cultivating entrepreneurship. Babson Park, MA: Babson Entrepreneurship Ecosystem Project, Babson College; 2011

[29] Leendertse J, Schrijvers M, Stam E. Measure twice, cut once: Entrepreneurial ecosystem metrics. Research Policy. 2021:1-27. DOI: 10.1016/j.respol.2021.104336

[30] Malecki EJ. Entrepreneurs, networks, and economic development: A review of recent research. In: Katz JA, editor. Advances in Entrepreneurship, Firm Emergence, and Growth. Greenwich, CT: JAI Press; 1997

[31] Tidd J, Bessant J, Pavitt K. Managing Innovation: Integrating Technological, Market and Organizational Change. 3rd ed. Chichester: John Wiley & Sons Ltd; 2005

[32] Oslo Manual. Guidelines for Collecting and Interpreting Innovation

Data. 3rd ed. A joint publication of OECD and Eurostat. Paris: OECD; 2005

[33] Adner R. Match your innovation strategy to your innovation ecosystem. Harvard Business Review. 2006;**84**(4):98-107

[34] Jackson DJ. What Is an Innovation Ecosystem. Arlington, VA: National Science Foundation; 2011

[35] Nambisan S, Baron RA. Entrepreneurship in innovation ecosystems: Entrepreneurs' self–regulatory processes and their implications for new venture success. Entrepreneurship Theory and Practice. 2013;**37**(5):1071-1097. DOI: 10.1111/j.1540-6520.2012.00519.x

[36] Autio E. Orchestrating ecosystems: A multi-layered framework. Innovation. 2021:1-14. DOI: 10.1080/14479338.2021.1919120

[37] Granstrand O, Holgersson M. Innovation ecosystems: A conceptual review and a new definition. Technovation. 2020;**90-91**:1-12. DOI: 10.1016/j.technovation.2019.102098

[38] Bittencourt BA, Santos DAG, Mignoni J. Resource orchestration in innovation ecosystems: A comparative study between innovation ecosystems at different stages of development. International Journal of Innovation - IJI, São Paulo. 2021;**9**(1):108-130. DOI: 10.5585/iji.v9i1.18076

[39] Thomas LDW, Sharapov D, Autio E. Linking entrepreneurial and innovation ecosystems: The case of AppCampus. In: Carayannis EG, Dagnino GB, Álvarez S, Faraci R, editors. Entrepreneurial Ecosystems and the Diffusion of Startups. Cheltenham: Edward Elgar Publishing; 2018. pp. 35-64. DOI: 10.4337/9781784710064.00008

[40] de Vasconcelos Gomes LA, Facin ALF, Salerno MS, Ikenami RK. Unpacking the innovation ecosystem construct: Evolution, gaps and trends. Technological Forecasting and Social Change, Elsevier. 2018;**136**(C):30-48

[41] Rabelo RJ, Bernus P. A holistic model of building innovation ecosystems. IFAC-Papers OnLine. 2015;**48**(3):2250-2257. DOI: 10.1016/j.ifacol.2015.06.423

[42] Bouncken RB, Kraus S. Entrepreneurial ecosystems in an interconnected world: Emergence, governance and digitalization. Review of Managerial Science. 2021;**16**:1-14. DOI: 10.1007/s11846-021-00444-1

[43] Belitski M, Godley A. The synergy approach to understand entrepreneurship and innovation ecosystem taxonomy. In: Tsvetkova A, Schmutzler J, Pugh R, editors. Entrepreneurial Ecosystems Meet Innovation Systems: Synergies, Policy Lessons and Overlooked Dimensions. Cheltenham, UK: Edward Elgar Publishing; 2020. pp. 152-169

[44] Feldman M, Siegel DS, Wright M. New developments in innovation and entrepreneurial ecosystems. Industrial and Corporate Change. 2019;**28**(4):817-826. DOI: 10.1093/icc/dtz031

[45] Burda YD, Volkova IO, Gavrikova EV. Meaningful analysis of innovation, business and entrepreneurial ecosystem concepts. Russian Management Journal. 2020;**18**(1):73-102. DOI: 10.21638/spbu18.2020.104

Chapter 5

Valuation and Capital Return as Inverse Problems

Petri P. Kärenlampi

Abstract

The capital return rate is the relative time change rate of value. Correspondingly, the current value can be produced in terms of value change rate divided by capital return rate. There is a variety of ways to approximate the expected capital return rate. These are briefly discussed. The approximation of the value change rate is still more variant, depending on the type of businesses discussed. A variety of businesses may appear within a firm, in which case the value change rates must be integrated. An example is provided of a real estate firm benefiting from the growth of multiannual plants of varying age. It is found that the application of a duration-dependent reference capital return rate increases the value increment rate of juvenile stands and decreases that of mature stands, however increasing the valuation result of both.

Keywords: capitalization, capital return rate, value increment rate, expected value

1. Introduction

The capital return rate is the relative time change rate of value. We choose to write

$$r(t) = \frac{d\kappa}{K(t)dt} \tag{1}$$

where κ in the numerator considers value growth, operative expenses, interests and amortizations, but neglects investments and withdrawals. In other words, it is the change of capitalization on an economic profit/loss basis. K in the denominator gives capitalization on a balance sheet basis, being directly affected by any investment or withdrawal.

A significant finding in Eq. (1) is that the capital return rate r depends not only on the value change rate $\frac{d\kappa}{dt}$, but also on the current valuation $K(t)$. Apparently, there is an intimate relationship between the capital return rate and the valuation. A fundamental question then is whether the valuation can be approached by inverting Eq. (1) as

$$K(t) = \frac{d\kappa}{r(t)dt} \tag{2}$$

Obviously, Eq. (2) is mathematically correct. However, in comparison with Eq. (1), it may appear less intuitive. While Eq. (1) provides the definition of capital return rate as a function of observable valuation, does Eq. (2) provide the definition of valuation as a function of observable capital return rate? Or does it possibly provide the definition of valuation as a function of the required capital return rate? Any of these interpretations is possible.

The quantities appearing on the right-hand side of Eq. (1) are observable in a variety of ways, including profit-loss—statement, balance sheet, and market valuation. As the right-hand side has been determined, the left-hand side is naturally known. However, this results in a circular definition in Eq. (2). Alternatively, the capital return rate appearing on the right-hand side of Eq. (2) can be determined from comparable reference investments.

The momentary definitions appearing in Eqs. (1) and (2) provide a highly simplified description of valuation and capital return rate. In reality, there is variability due to a number of factors. Enterprises often contain businesses distributed to a variety of production lines, geographic areas, and markets. In addition, quantities appearing in Eqs. (1) and (2) are not necessarily completely known but may contain probabilistic scatter. Correspondingly, the expected values of capital return rate and valuation can be written as

$$\langle r(t)\rangle = \frac{\int p_{\frac{d\kappa}{dt}} \frac{d\kappa}{dt} d\frac{d\kappa}{dt}}{\int p_K K(t) dK} = \frac{\int p_{\frac{d\kappa}{dt}} r(t) K(t) d\frac{d\kappa}{dt}}{\int p_K K(t) dK} \tag{3}$$

and

$$\langle K(t)\rangle = \int p_K K(t) dK = \int p_K \frac{d\kappa/dt}{r(t)} dK \tag{4}$$

where p_i corresponds to the probability density of quantity i. It is found that while the capital return rate and the capitalization are simply invertible in the absence of any variation (Eqs. (1) and (2)), the same is not the case in the presence of variation, either deterministic or probabilistic (Eqs. (3) and (4)). Here, it is worth noting that the capital return rate in the denominator of Eq. (4) obviously tends to a "reference" capital return rate, rather than a directly observed one.

In the remaining part of this chapter, we will first discuss the practical implementation of the determination of capital return rate and firm value using Eqs. (3) and (4) in the case of a real estate firm benefiting from the growth of multiannual plant stands of varying age. Then, we will discuss the determination of the values of the quantities appearing in Eqs. (3) and (4), as well as factors contributing to them. Finally, a few applications are discussed, as well as interpolation techniques.

2. Application to stands of multiannual plants

In this section, the determination of capital return rate and enterprise value is discussed in the case of a real estate firm benefiting from the growth of multiannual plant stands of varying ages. Conducting a change of variables in Eqs. (3) and (4) results as

$$\langle r(t)\rangle = \frac{\int p_a(t) \frac{d\kappa}{dt}(a,t) da}{\int p_a(t) K(a,t) da} = \frac{\int p_a(t) r(a,t) K(a,t) da}{\int p_a(t) K(a,t) da} \tag{5}$$

and

$$\langle K(t)\rangle = \int p_a(t)K(a,t)da = \int p_a(t)\frac{\frac{d\kappa}{dt}(a,t)}{r(a,t)}da \tag{6}$$

where a refers to stand age. Again, the capital return rate in the denominator of Eq. (6) rather refers to a reference rate than a directly observed one.

It is found from Eqs. (5) and (6) that the probability density of stand age is a function of time, and correspondingly, the capital return rate, as well as the estate value, evolves in time. A significant simplification would appear if the probability densities appearing on the right-hand side of Eqs. (5) and (6) would not change along with time. Within forestry, such a situation would be denoted "normal forest principle." corresponding to evenly distributed stand age determining relevant stand properties [1].

$$\langle r(t)\rangle = \frac{\int \frac{d\kappa}{dt}(a)da}{\int K(a)da} = \frac{\int r(a)K(a)da}{\int K(a)da} \tag{7}$$

and

$$\langle K(t)\rangle = p_a\int K(a,t)da = p_a\int \frac{\frac{d\kappa}{dt}(a,t)}{r(a,t)}da \tag{8}$$

The "normal forest principle" is rather useful when considering silvicultural practices, but seldom applies to the valuation of real-life real estate firms, with generally non-uniform stand age distribution. However, it has recently been shown [2] that the principle is not necessary for the simplification of Eqs. (5) and (6) into (7) and (8). This happens by focusing on a single stand, instead of an entire estate or enterprise, and considering that time proceeds linearly. Then, the probability density function p (a) is constant within an interval [0, τ]. Correspondingly, it has vanished from Eq. (7) and appeared outside of the integral in Eq. (8).

The topic of this chapter, however, is firm valuation. As the relatively simple Eqs. (7) and (8) are useful in the design of silvicultural practices, firm valuation typically happens at a specific instant of time, and the probability density $p(a)$ generally is non-uniform. Correspondingly, Eqs. (5) and (6) must be applied. Fortunately, $p(a)$ usually is known for any property where recent inventory results are available. It is further fortunate that Eqs. (4), (6), and (8) contain simple summations, unlike Eqs. (3), (5), and (7).

3. Determination of stand capitalization

There is a variety of methods to determine the value K appearing in Eqs. (3)–(6). In the case of an incorporated company or a firm with equivalent reporting, the value can be found from the balance sheet. Such an outcome does depend on applied accounting practices. On the other hand, the value can be determined as a market value. The latter is straightforward in the case of publicly listed companies, or other companies with the established share trading records. A third alternative for firm value determination is the computation of an "intrinsic value," considering the prognosticated future development of the firm [3–5].

In the case of a real estate firm benefiting from the growth of multiannual plants of varying age, the value K within any stand may be approached as the sum of the value of the plants on the stand, the value of bare land, and the value of non-amortized investments. Such computation is problematic if non-mature plants do not have any immediate sale value. In such a case, it is not uncommon to determine stand value by discounting expected future revenues [6–9]. The discount rate is sometimes taken arbitrarily, but often it can be determined as an internal rate of return [10].

We here provide a few examples of the determination of the value of forest stands by interpolation. It is not uncommon that planted seedlings may require several years to mature to young trees of commercial value. However, during those years, expected revenues become closer in time. Correspondingly, it would be unrealistic to assume the growth of saplings would not add value. The capitalization, including such an additional expected value, could be approximated by some kind of a smoothing function. One possibility could be

$$k(a) = \frac{1}{\tau - a} \int_{a}^{\tau} K(t) \exp\left[r(t) * (a - t)\right] dt \tag{9}$$

where r(t) is the capital return rate at stand age t. A simpler version would be

$$k(a) = \frac{1}{\tau - a} \int_{a}^{\tau} K(t) \exp\left[\langle r \rangle * (a - t)\right] dt \tag{10}$$

Both of the above equations converge to terminal capitalization $k(\tau) = K(\tau)$, regardless of the capital return rate $r(t)$ or $\langle r \rangle$. However, there is no guarantee of any definite convergence in a newly established stand. Such convergence $k(initial) = K(initial)$ could be approached by fitting an internal rate of return i, which provides convergence. That would correspond to assuming that the bare land value includes any additional expectation value for a newly established stand, resulting as

$$k(a) = \frac{1}{\tau - a} \int_{a}^{\tau} K(t) \exp\left[i * (a - t)\right] dt \tag{11}$$

It might be possible to determine capitalization indirectly by discounting revenue. This would result as

$$k(a) = BL + \int_{a}^{\tau} R(t) \exp\left[j * (a - t)\right] dt \tag{12}$$

where BL denotes bare land value, and $R(t)$ net revenue at time t. Again, the discount rate j shall be fitted for convergence $k(initial) = K(initial)$.

The functionality of Eqs. (11) and (12) are investigated in **Figure 1**, in the case of a spruce stand established with 1800 saplings/ha, and a wooded stand observed at the age of 35 years. The former initial condition is based on the early application of a growth model on saplings stands [11, 12], the latter on the observations of the wooded stand [12, 13]. The former shows a positive additional expectation value of trees for

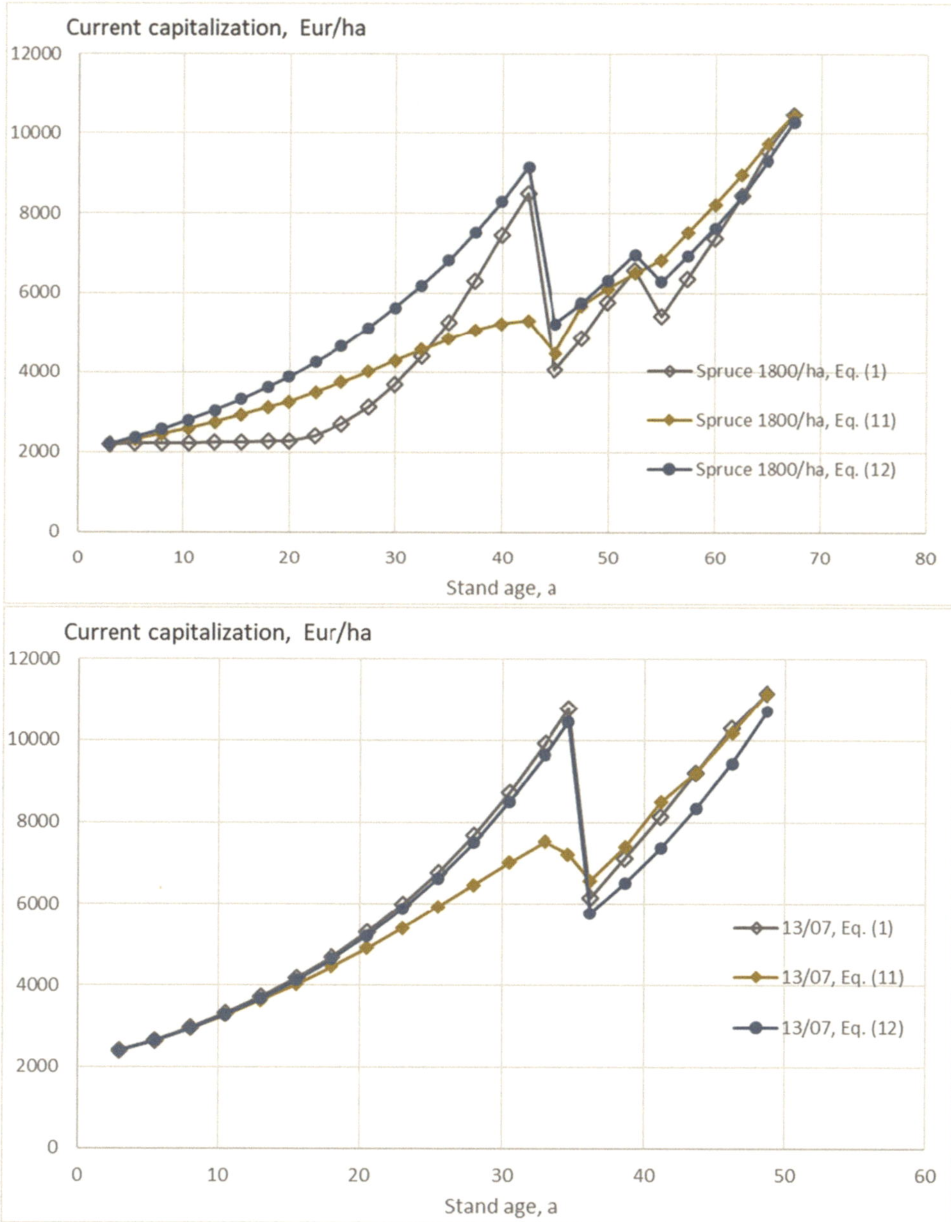

Figure 1.
Capitalization, as appearing in Eq. (1), as well as smoothed capitalization according to Eqs. (11) and (12), in the case of the two example stands. (a) (above) shows a spruce stand established with 1800 saplings/hectare. (b) (below) shows a spruce stand first observed at the age of 35 years.

young stands and after thinnings. If such additional values would be considered, microeconomically optimal rotation ages would be affected. However, Eq. (11) results as the additional value being negative before the first thinning. It is not known how the negative additional expectation value should be considered in management. Within the wooded stand observed at 35 years of age, the additional expectation value of trees of young stands according to Eq. (11) would be negative, being slightly positive only after thinning. Eq. (12) would indicate zero additional value before thinning and somewhat negative after thinning. An explanation for the latter is that regeneration expenses are carried in the balance sheet until the end of the rotation. This results in the capitalization at mature age being greater than the sum of discounted terminal revenue and bare land value.

Figure 1a indicates that in the case of the early application of the growth model, internal rate of return-based interpolation could be useful in the determination of young stand capitalization. In the absence of such adjustment, there would be a negligible value increment for a period of two decades. Eq. (12) can be straightforwardly applied by substituting k(a) from in place of K(a) in Eqs. (5), (6), (7), or (8). However, interpolation is possible only after an initial treatment schedule has been designed using Eqs. (5) or (7). Correspondingly, Eq. (12) must be used iteratively with the other equations.

On the other hand, in the case of **Figure 1b**, interpolation of capitalization appears irrelevant. A natural reason is that the stand has been first observed at the age of 35 years. The capitalization from the stand establishment to the time of observation already has been approximated by exponential interpolation. Correspondingly, results based on the observations of wooded stands do not appear to be in the need of any further interpolation.

4. Determination of a reference capital return rate

In money market theory, increased duration of commitments tends to increase the risk experienced by the borrower [14–16]. However, in **Figure 1**, the discount rates do not depend on the delay time of revenues. This could be corrected by introducing a delay-dependent discount rate. One possibility is a spot discount rate

$$j = \ln\left(u + \frac{d}{s}\right) \tag{13}$$

where d is time to maturity, and u and s are constants. Now, the constants u and s can be adjusted to gain the correspondence $k(initial) = K(initial)$ in Eq. (12). On the other hand, it is only the constant u that determines the discount rate at maturity and that can be determined through matching terminal discount rate to terminal capital return rate, determined as the ratio of terminal value increment rate to terminal capitalization. The outcome, in terms of stand capitalization, is shown in **Figure 2**. At intermediate stand ages, the capitalization becomes higher when Eq. (13) is applied. This is because the revenue is less severely discounted close to maturity. Greater discount rate close to the stand establishment then ensures the correspondence $k(initial) = K(initial)$.

5. Determination of stand value increment rate

There is a variety of methods to determine the value increment rate $^{d\kappa}/_{dt}$ appearing in Eqs. (1)–(8). In the case of an incorporated company, or a firm with equivalent reporting, the value increment rate can be found from a(n annual, quarterly, or prognosticated) profit/loss—statement. The outcome does depend on applied accounting practices.

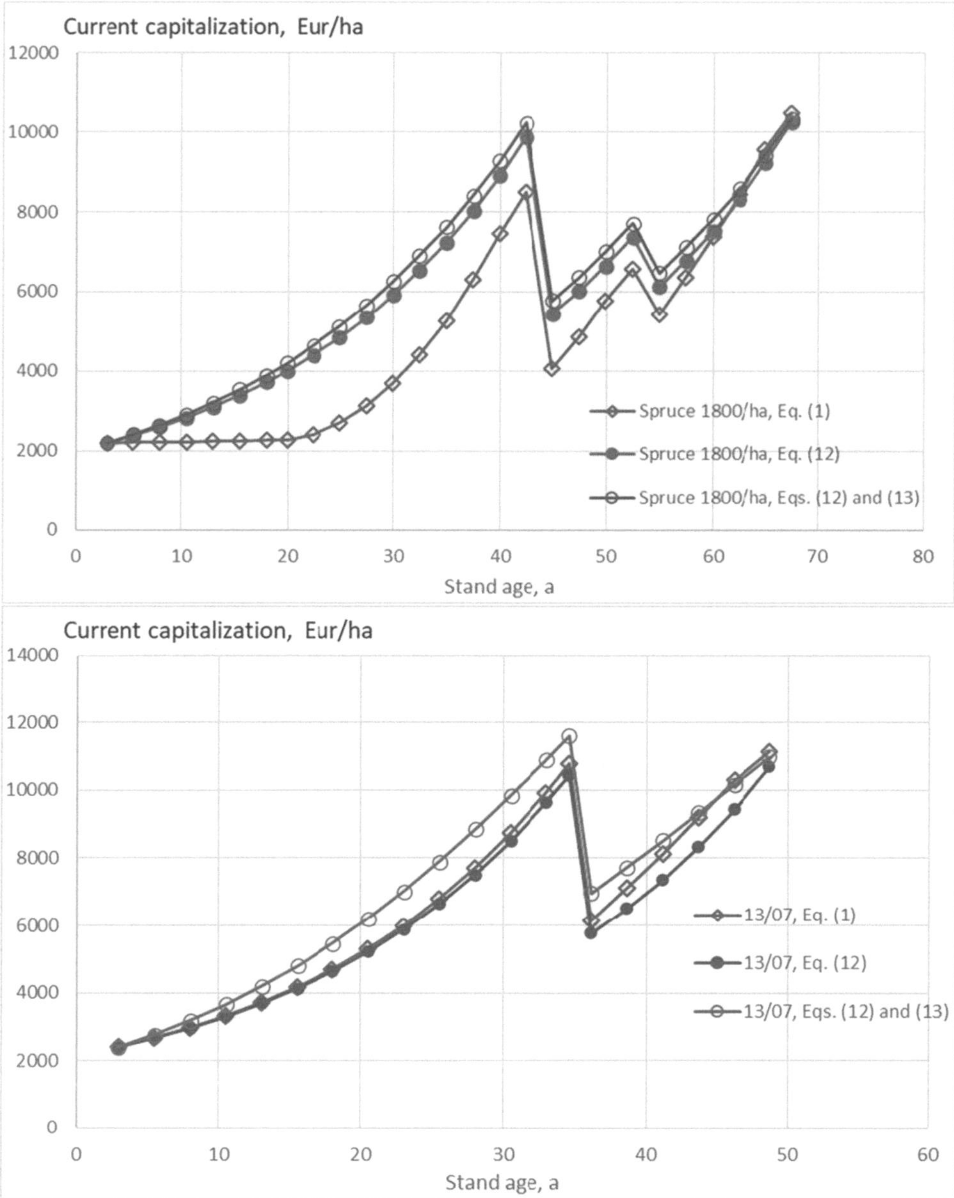

Figure 2.
Capitalization, as appearing in Eq. (1), as well as smoothed capitalization according to Eq. (12) with constant discount rate and (12) together with (13), in the case of the two example stands. (a) (above) shows a spruce stand established with 1800 saplings/hectare. (b) (below) shows a spruce stand first observed at the age of 35 years.

In the case of a real estate firm benefiting from the growth of multiannual plants of varying age, the value increment rate within any stand may be approached by the value increment rate of the plants on the stand, possibly complemented with the increment rate of bare land value. The value increment rate generally is constituted on volumetric increment on the one hand and increment of volumetrically specific value on the other hand [17]. Again, such computation is problematic if non-mature plants do not have any immediate sales value.

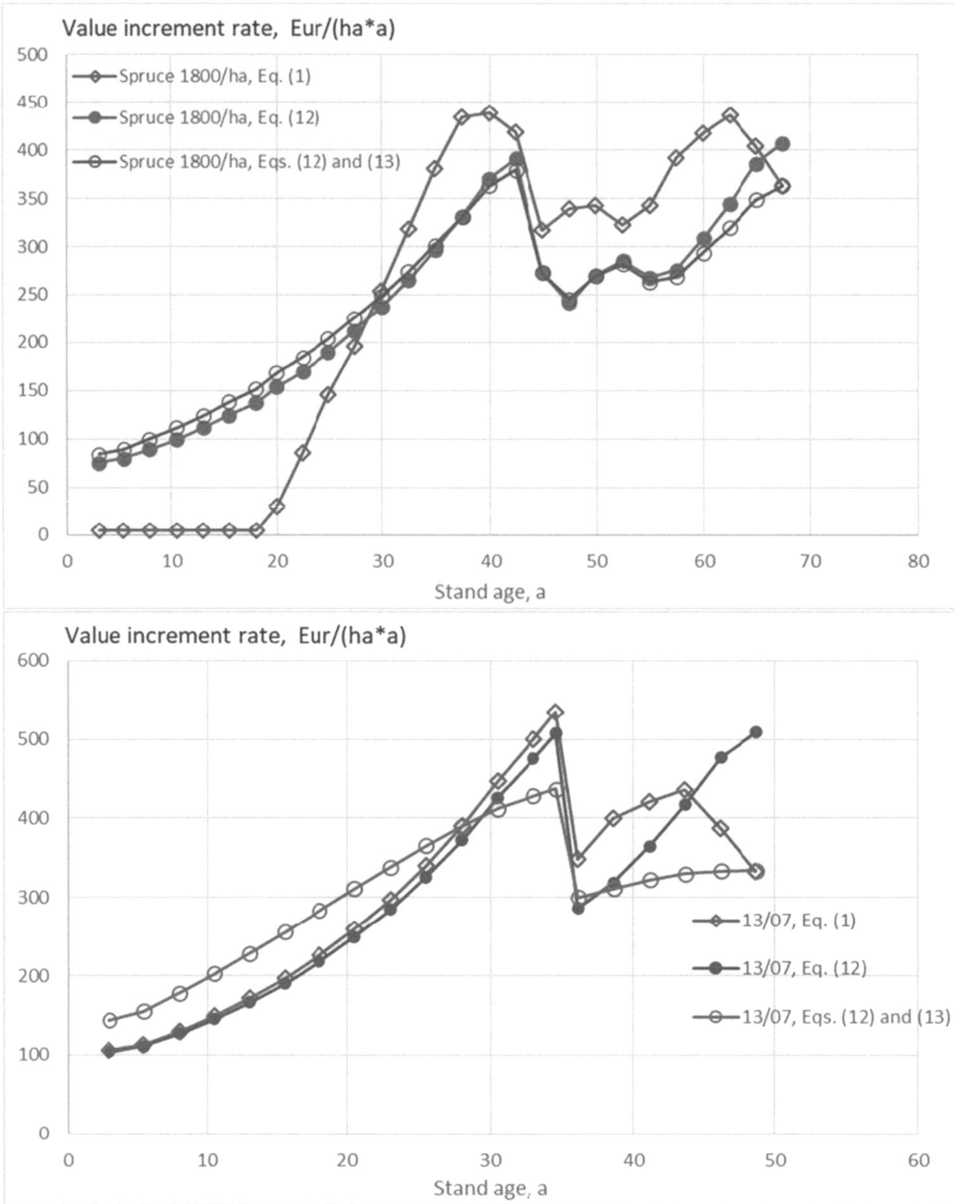

Figure 3.
Annual monetary value increment rate, as appearing in Eq. (1), as well as Eq. (12) with constant discount rate and (12) together with (13), in the case of the two example stands. Fig. 3a (above) shows a spruce stand established with 1800 saplings/hectare. Fig. 3b (below) shows a spruce stand first observed at the age of 35 years.

Figure 3 shows the annual value increment rate per hectare, determined using three different methods. Firstly, the annual value increment is determined directly using the growth model, as often applied in Eq. (1). With the initial condition based on the early application of a growth model on saplings stands (**Figure 3a**), the initial value increment rate is small, increasing rapidly later. Value increment rate based on discounting of revenue with the constant discount rate (Eq. (12)) is smoother, even if not monotonic. Incorporating the delay-dependent discount rate (Eq. (13)) increases the value increment rate at a young age and reduces it at a mature age (**Figure 3**). Similar trends are observable in the case of the example stand first observed at the age of 35 years, except for early stand development according to Eq. (1) is similar to the discounting result with the constant discount rate (Eq. (12) (**Figure 3b**).

The relative annual value increment rate can be readily found by normalizing the monetary increment rate of **Figure 3** with the capitalization appearing in **Figure 2**. The outcome is in **Figure 4**. With the initial condition based on the early application

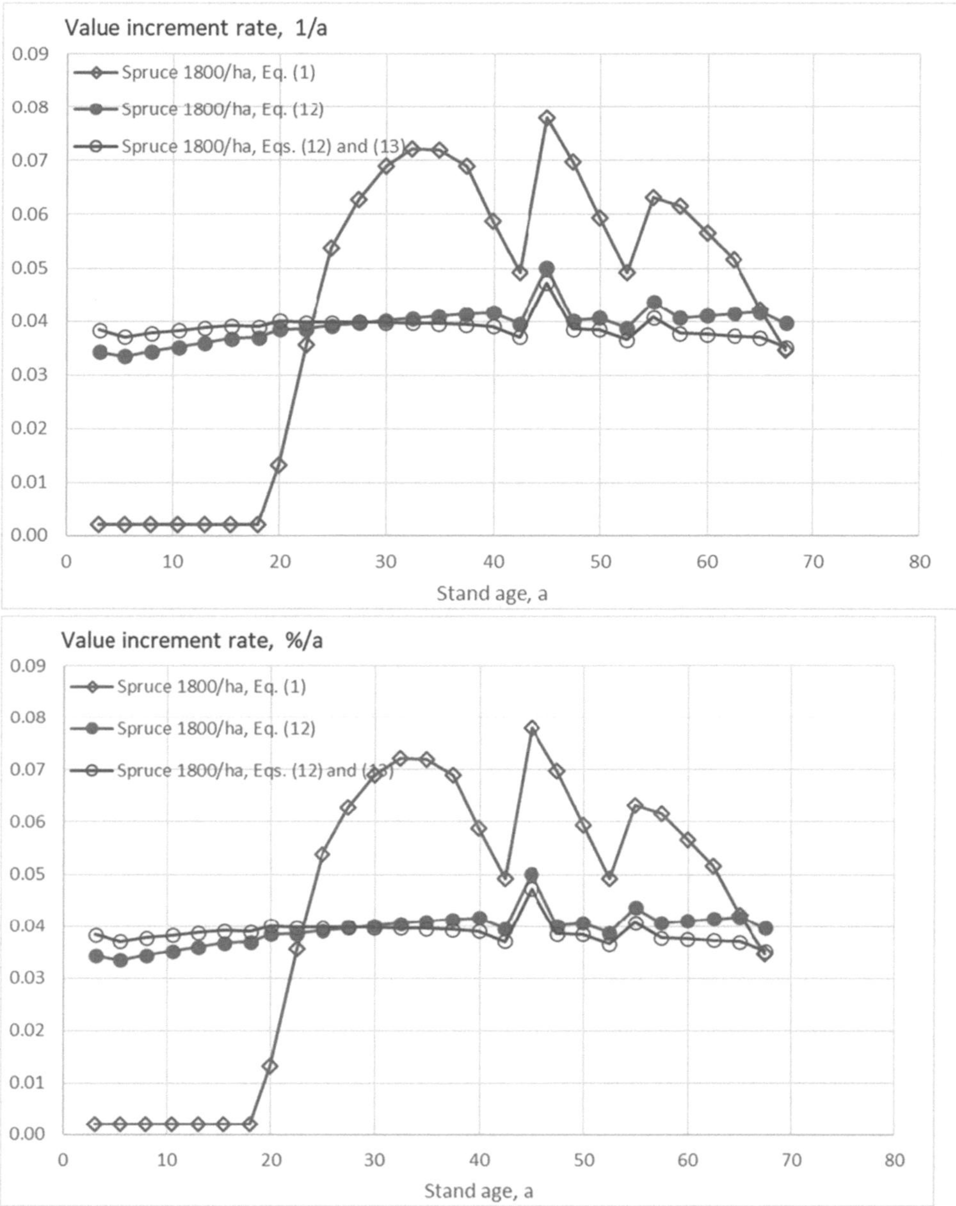

Figure 4.
Annual relative value increment rate, as appearing in Eq. (1), as well as Eq. (12) with constant discount rate and (12) together with (13), in the case of the two example stands. (a) (above) shows a spruce stand established with 1800 saplings/hectare. (b) (below) shows a spruce stand first observed at the age of 35 years.

of a growth model on saplings stands (**Figure 4a**), direct application of the growth model induces a volatile relative value increment rate. On the contrary, capitalization determined by discounting revenue yields stationary value increment rates, except for increases after thinnings. Again, delay-dependent discount rate (Eq. (13)) induces larger value increments at a young age and lower at a mature age. The latter effect is more pronounced in the case of the example stand observed at the wooded state (**Figure 4b**).

6. Further valuation attempts

It is of interest whether Eqs. (4) and (13) can be combined for the valuation of an individual stand. A possibility is

$$K(a) = \frac{\int_a^\tau {}^{d\kappa}\!/_{dt} \exp\left[j(t-a)*(a-t)\right]dt}{(\tau - a)*r(a)} \tag{14}$$

where reference capital return rate r(a) comprises a numerical solution of Eqs. (12) and (13), appearing in **Figure 4**. The result is shown in **Figure 5**. The reference capital return rate according to Eq. (13) increasing with increasing time to maturity, it is found that mature stands show greater value than the reference curves, whereas juvenile stands show lower value. Eq. (14), however, has an obvious deficiency: The value estimate does match the known terminal value but not the initial value.

The obvious deficiency in Eq. (14) can be simply corrected. The reference capital return rate $r(a)$ can be modified, however possibly retaining the simple form of Eq. (13). Eq. (14) can possibly be further simplified by using the same reference rate in the discounting of the value increments. The outcome would be

$$K(a) = \frac{\int_a^\tau {}^{d\kappa}\!/_{dt} \exp\left[l(t-a)*(a-t)\right]dt}{(\tau - a)*l(a)} \tag{15}$$

However, there is another deficiency in Eq. (14) and in **Figure 5**. The approximated stand value before the first thinning appears lower than the immediate sales value of the trees. This deficiency does not become corrected by Eq. (15). Correspondingly, Eqs. (14) and (15) cannot be considered appropriate.

7. Discussion

The capital return rate and firm valuation have been discussed as inverse problems. The invertibility is obvious in the absence of probabilistic or deterministic scatter. In the presence of scatter, the invertibility is less straightforward. However, the firm valuation corresponds to a simple sum of units or compartments according to Eqs. (4), (6), and (8).

A real estate firm benefiting from the growth of multiannual plant stands of varying age was discussed as a practical example. Again, the total value is a simple sum of the values of compartments, which transfers the focus to the valuation of

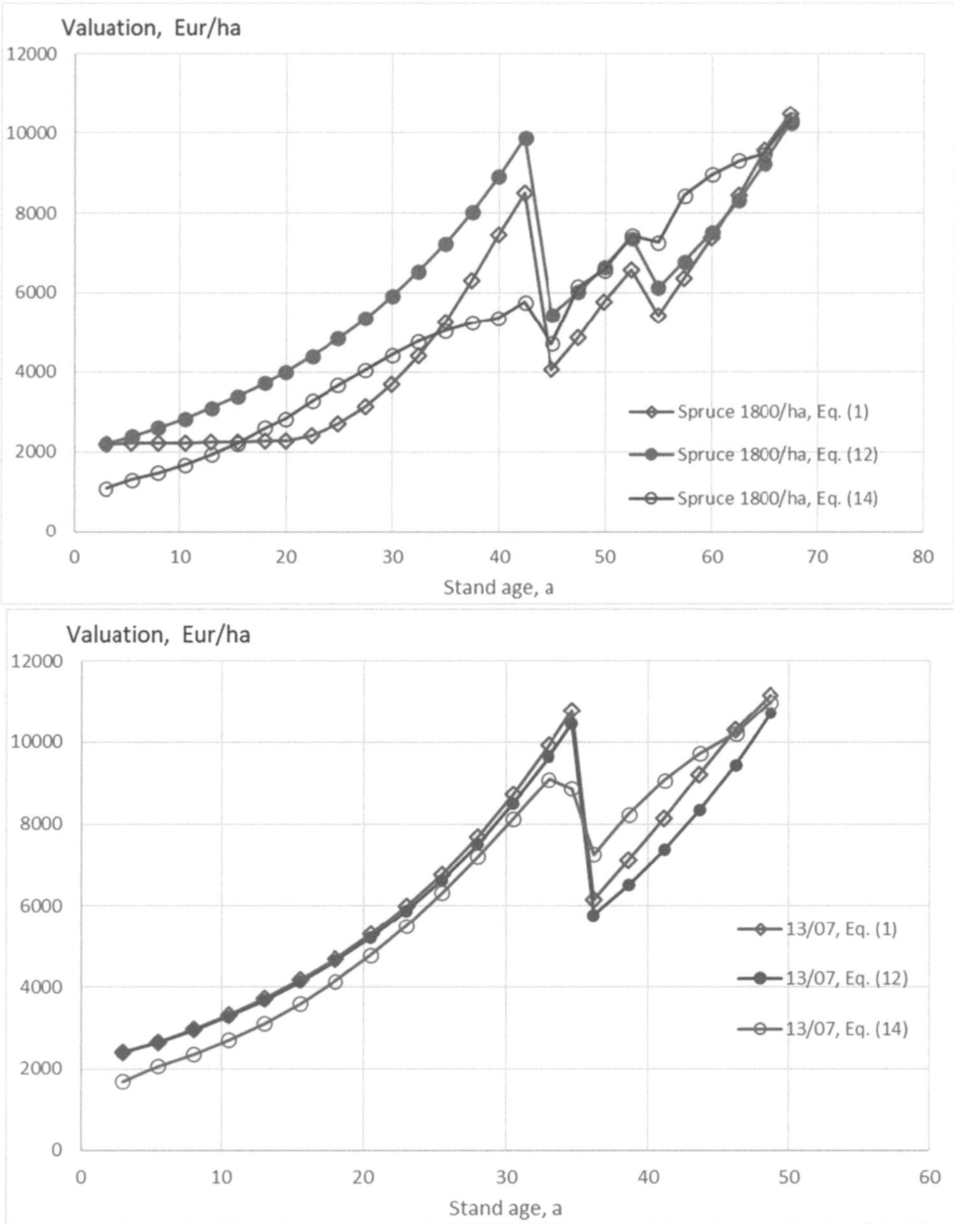

Figure 5.
Capitalization, as appearing in Eq. (1), as well as Eq. (12) with constant discount rate and (12) together with (13), in the case of the two example stands.

individual stands. Young stands with small immediate sales value, or other stands expected to increase in value rapidly in the future, appear to be a problem in stand valuation. Attempts in discounting future capitalization appear to be unsuccessful but attempts in discounting revenue successful. Such discounting appears necessary if the value of the plants is determined through high-resolution observation or computation. Observation of more mature stands, along with interpolation to more juvenile stands, takes care of such interpolation in value (**Figures 1**, **2**, and **5**).

Discounting of revenue with constant discount rate, however, appears to be unsatisfactory since it produces stand values slightly lower than the immediate sales value (**Figures 1, 2,** and **5**). This can be corrected by introducing a discount rate that considers the duration effect (or time-to-maturity), according to Eq. (13). Such discount rate slightly increases stand value estimates (**Figure 2**). It increases value increment rate at a young age and reduces it at a mature age (**Figures 3** and **4**).

This chapter, after introducing generic expressions for valuation and capital return as inverse problems, has discussed the valuation of two example cases in a restricted manner. In other words, the initial value and the terminal value are taken as known quantities, and value evolution between these extremes has been interpolated. Such a restricted treatment has some definite benefits: Internal consistency of the results can be relatively easily verified. An important tool in the verification is the non-interpolated sum of value components generally used in Eq. (1). In the case of a forestry firm, that might become

$$K(a) = \textit{bare land value} + \textit{value of trees} + \textit{value of non-amortized investments} \quad (16)$$

The last term in Eq. (16) depends on investment intensity, as well as the amortization schedule. For the purposes of an internal consistency criterion, we define a *reduced current capitalization* as

$$K'(a) = \textit{bare land value} + \textit{value of trees} \quad (17)$$

Approximations of capitalization established in Eqs. (9) to (12) are designed to include expectations of forthcoming value increment. Consequently, one can take for granted

$$k(a) \geq K'(a) \quad (18)$$

The brief examination above revealed that Eqs. (9), (10), (11), and (14) generally do not satisfy this internal consistency criterion and must thus be rejected. Eq. (12), applied with or without Eq. (13), often does satisfy the consistency criterion. However, this does not happen in all circumstances. Particularly, Eq. (12) with a constant discount rate fails to comply with Eq. (18) with large rotation ages, where the value increment rate becomes essentially non-exponential.

Other kinds of problems relate to Eq. (13). First, there are circumstances where the parameter s turns negative. In particular, this happens in the case of young, productive stands with growth only slightly differing from exponential. Consequently, increased duration of commitments tends to decrease the discount rate or, in other words, invert the yield curve.

Another issue related to Eq. (13) is that it is sensitive to short-range disturbances close to maturity. In particular, recent thinning typically increases the relative value increment rate. Consequently, parameter u in Eq. (13) increases. The estimated capitalization then decreases, and the expected value of capital return rate according to Eqs. (3), (5), or (7) increases. This suggests terminal clear-cutting soon after thinning —a result which obviously is a computational artifact. Instead, Eq. (12) with a constant discount rate appears to remain a valid estimate, provided the internal consistency criterion of Eq. (18) is satisfied.

As mentioned, this chapter has discussed the valuation of two example cases in a restricted manner. A less restricted treatment might open further avenues. A particular possibility might be the introduction of a variety of reference capital return rates in the denominator of Eqs. (2), (4), (6), and (8). Linking the reference rate to alternative investments like interest instruments or shares of listed companies would significantly change valuations—not only intermediate valuations but also the initial and terminal values. The initial value would likely be more affected since the proportion of the bare land value is greater than in the terminal value, the latter including the terminal sales value of mature timber.

Acknowledgements

This work was partially supported by Niemi Foundation. Prof. Dr. Lauri Mehtätalo is gratefully acknowledged for fruitful discussions.

Author details

Petri P. Kärenlampi
Lehtoi Research, Finland

*Address all correspondence to: petri.karenlampi@professori.fi

References

[1] Leslie AJ. A review of the concept of the normal forest. Australian Forestry. 1966;**30**:139-147. DOI: 10.1080/00049158.1966.10675407

[2] Kärenlampi PP. Two Sets of Initial Conditions on Boreal Forest Carbon Storage Economics. Accepted to PLOS Climate. 2021

[3] Tiwari R. Intrinsic value estimates and its accuracy: Evidence from Indian manufacturing industry. Future Business Journal. 2016;**2**(2):138-151. DOI: 10.1016/j.fbj.2016.10.001

[4] Tanjung G. The applications of discount cash flow, abnormal earning, and relative valuation approach. In: (Firm Intrinsic Value Analysis Pada Perusahaan BUMN) Conference: Seminar Nasional Kewirausahaan dan Inovasi Bisnis IVAt: Universitas, Tarumanegara. Bandung, Indonesia: Universitas Widyatama; 2014

[5] Carlin S. How To Calculate Intrinsic Value (Formula – Excel template & AMZN Example). Available from: https://svencarlin.com/how-to-calculate-intrinsic-value-formula/ [Accessed September 14, 2021]

[6] Kilkki P, Väisänen U. Determination of the optimum cutting policy for the forest stand by means of dynamic programming. Acta Forestalia Fennica. 1969;**102**:1-29

[7] Haight RG, Monserud RA. Optimizing any-aged management of mixed-species stands. II: Effects of decision criteria. Forest Science. 1990;**36**:125-144

[8] Pukkala T, Lähde E, Laiho O. Optimizing the structure and management of uneven-sized stands in Finland. Forestry. 2010;**83**:129-142

[9] Tahvonen O. Optimal structure and development of uneven-aged Norway spruce forests. Canadian Journal of Forest Research. 2011;**41**:2389-2402

[10] Kärenlampi PP. Wealth accumulation in rotation forestry–Failure of the net present value optimization? PLoS One. 2019;**14**:e0222918. DOI: 10.1371/journal.pone.0222918

[11] Kärenlampi PP. Capital return rate and carbon storage on forest estates of three boreal tree species. Sustainability. 2021;**13**(12):6675. DOI: 10.3390/su13126675

[12] Kärenlampi PP. Two sets of initial conditions on boreal forest carbon storage economics. Preprint. 2021:2021070439. DOI: 10.20944/preprints202107.0439.v2

[13] Kärenlampi PP. Diversity of carbon storage economics in fertile boreal spruce (Picea Abies) estates. Sustainability. 2021;**13**:560. Available from: https://www.mdpi.com/2071-1050/13/2/560

[14] Bouchaud J-P, Potters M. Théorie des Risques Financiers (Saclay: Aléa). In: (Engl. transl. 2000) Theory of Financial Risks. Cambridge: Cambridge University Press; 1997. Available from: http://web.math.ku.dk/~rolf/Klaus/bouchaud-book.ps.pdf

[15] Brealey RA, Myers SC, Allen F. Principles of Corporate Finance. Tenth ed. New York, NY: McGraw-Hill Irwin; 2011

[16] Fabozzi FJ. Capital Markets: Institutions, Instruments, and Risk Management. Cambridge, Massachusetts: MIT Press; 2015

[17] Kärenlampi PP. The effect of empirical log yield observations on carbon storage economics. Forests. 2020; **11**:1312

Chapter 6

The "Lateral Transshipment" is a Cooperative Tool for Optimizing the Profitability of a Distribution System

Elleuch Fadoi

Abstract

In this chapter, we discuss a network consisting of a distribution center (or central depot) and two retailers who serve customers. D_1 and D_2 represent, respectively, the demands of retailer 1 and 2. We assume that the demand D_i (i = 1, 2) at retailer i follows a normal distribution with mean μ_i and standard deviation σ_i (known). This analysis makes it possible to assess the effect of emergency transshipment both at the level of the Average Global Profit and of the Average Global Desservice Rate. In this chapter, we consider a centralized one-echelon supply chain with two-retailers selling products and facing stochastic demand.

Keywords: transshipment policies, complete-pooling, partial-pooling, simulation, vendor-managed inventory, supply chain management, partial-pooling threshold

1. Introduction

Effective supply chain management is now recognized as a key element of competitiveness and success in most industrial enterprises. However, since the network that makes up the supply chain is usually too complex to analyze and optimize on a large scale, it is often preferable to focus on smaller parts of the system so as to gain a full understanding of its characteristics and performance. Each component of the same level manages its stock in a independent to each other. Such attention is paid to this network because of its complexity (uncertainty of demand, lead time, etc.) which increases significantly. The overall performance of the storage network, whether evaluated in economic terms or in terms of customer service, can be significantly improved if sites (retailers, outlets, stores) work together in this random environment. Collaboration between sites is defined as cooperation where collaborating sites share their stocks when needed. Generally, the collaboration is made laterally (in the same echelon) from a site which has a surplus of stock to another which faces a shortage of stock: what is called lateral transshipment. Collaboration could be an effective way to improve the logistics performance of the company without any need for additional cost. As the cost of lateral transfer of items between sites is generally much lower than the cost of shortage and the cost of emergency delivery from central warehouse, and the lateral transfer time is shorter than the regular replenishment lead time, so the collaboration could reduce the total system cost and improve the level of service for customers. There are two types of collaboration: emergency collaboration and preventive collaboration. The goal of the emergency collaboration, which takes place after receipt of the demand, is to address current disruptions in inventory. While preventive collaboration, which is done before receiving customer demand, aims to reduce the risk of having stock-out in the future. Collaboration can also be classified according to the quantity to be transferred: there is full collaboration where the site offers all its available stock when another site faces a stock-out and partial collaboration where the site keeps part of the stock to cover future demand.

Several quantitative decision support models are proposed in the literature to study the impact of lateral transfer between sites. These models can be classified according to several characteristics: (1) the structure of the network (2) the type of optimization model.

In the articles reviewed [Shahab Derhami et al. [1], Wong et al. [2]], there are at least six important criteria which are taken into consideration in a comprehensive study of the subject: (1) the number of collaborators in the group, (2) the time of replenishment from the central warehouse, (3) the profile of the request, (4) the time (before or after receipt of the request) and the purpose of the collaboration (emergency or preventive), (5) repairability of stored items and (6) performance measures (cost or level of service).

A large number of works focus in their research on the type of lateral transshipment, ie. Emergency transhipment or preventive transhipment.

Herer et al. [3] analyzed the emergency lateral transshipment strategy between two-retailers and found this last can simultaneously improve lightness and agility. Paterson et al. [4] and Noham and Tzur [5] respectively developed a quasi-myopic approach and a simple heuristic algorithm. Van et al. [6] have presented models where preventive collaboration takes place before receipt of the request in order to have a better distribution of stock available between the different collaborators.

Archibald et al. [7] studied an inventory system considering that basic stock is ordered, while the decision to place an emergency order from the warehouse or to use lateral transfer depends on the costs, the time remaining in the warehouse. The period and inventory available in the alternative site. Relaxing the hypothesis of the instant central warehouse replenishment time considerably complicates the mathematical analysis of the network because of the interrelationships between demand, quantities to be transferred and stock in transit. In particular, if the optimal transfer strategy should take into account both on-hand and on-order inventory, implying that state space should be increased. In addition, full collaboration assuming that the lead time is negligible and where the costs across the sites are the same, is not necessarily optimal when the lead time is positive. Therefore, the decision space is more complex and the exact model becomes intractable even in the simple case (two-retailers). Li et al. [8] aim to study the effect of preventive lateral transhipment on the quantities ordered in a two-echelons inventory system. Liao et al. [9] studied a comparison between side transfer and emergency order options. The sharing is done in a bidirectional way to coordinate the transhipment quantities. Olsson [10] studied a lateral transshipment policy for a two-retailers inventory system with a positive transshipment delay. A more sophisticated transhipment policy has been developed, the results of which show that it is worthwhile to reduce transhipment times. Torabi et al. [11] analyzed a problem of an inventory system in an e-commerce environment with complete-pooling. A mixed integer programming model has been formulated and solved to minimize logistics costs. Lee and Park [12] studied an inventory model with two retailers and a single supplier with uncertain capacity. By applying lateral transshipment, they found that a transshipment price may be able to coordinate the supply chain. Feng et al. [13] discussed a dynamic problem of preventive lateral transshipment in a centralized inventory system based on Markov decision making. They used simulation to study the inventory system with significant reorder time and different costs. The authors conclude that full collaboration is less expensive than partial collaboration. They also provided approximations for on-hand inventory, shortage inventory, and transfer inventory as well as heuristics to determine a near-optimal reorder point solution under full collaboration. Silbermayr et al. [14] investigated the problem of emergency lateral transshipment with environmental sustainability. The research of Nakandala et al. [15] focuses on the study of an emergency lateral transshipment model for perishable products in a fresh produce supply chain. This research is concerned with applying a more comprehensive transshipment decision method to help the practitioner make profitable decisions. Timajchi et al. [16] discussed an inventory flow problem with a transshipment of pharmaceutical items. Feng et al. [17] analyzed such advanced research to study emergency lateral transshipment and preventive transshipment in a comparable partially delayed setting. Dehghani and Abbasi [18] propose a policy of emergency transshipment of perishable foodstuffs in supply chains. They developed a heuristic solution to calculate performance metrics. Timajchi et al. [19] analyzed deterioration in pharmaceuticals and proposed a side-shift option to meet demand while simultaneously minimizing costs and accidental losses. Yi et al. [20] found the optimal emergency transshipment and replenishment decisions within a decentralized inventory system framework. They build a multistep stochastic model that captures the uncertainty of demand and changing customer behavior.

2. Modeling mathematical

We have studied the periodic storage policy (R, S_i) for each retailer *1* and *2*. The stock control period, noted *R*, is made up of *T* time intervals separated by two successive customer requests for each retailer *i, With i = 1, 2.*

According to this policy, at the end of each review period R (assumed equal to 28 days, according to, Emel and Lena [21], if the stock position of retailer *i* (noted, PS_{iT} = Stock available − Demand) goes down in below a given value, called the replenishment level and noted S_i, a replenishment order is launched from the central warehouse so as to bring this stock position back to S_i, The order is received at the 'end of the supply period L.

We are targeting to improve the global profitability of stock system composed of two retailers by minimizing the Desservice rate of each site by decreasing the quantity out of stock. This result in the improvement of the Average Global Profit in the whole inventory system this can be done by applying the cooperation between these retailers which is called by the transshipment, either by the application of the policy of transhipment: "Complete-Pooling" or "Partial-Pooling". Each time we modified the threshold of the "Partial-Pooling" transshipment policy, the periodicity *T* and the unit cost of transshipment. We consider a distribution system consisting of two retailers no-identical *(i* = 1, 2) owned or operated by the same entity and one manufacturer that sells to these retailers in a single period. Following the newsvendor scenario, the central depot owner needs to decide, for retailer *n*, a no negative order quantity Q_i, before observing demand D_i, with i = 1,2.

To solve this type of problem, we can apply the “Without-Transshipment” policy, that is to say, when the retailer falls into an out-of-stock position, he demands the quantity of central deposit missing to satisfy customer demand, or, by applying the “With-Transshipment” policy, by adopting a relationship between the retailers who are in the same line to minimize the stock shortage and meet a random demand. In this chapter we will try to find the most appealing controversy that aims to maximize the expected Average Global Profit and minimize as much as possible the Average Global Desservice Rate.

The quantity of supply within time intervals T is then expressed by the Eq. (1).

$$Q_i = \begin{cases} S_i - PS_{iT} & if PS_{iT} \leq S_i \\ 0 & Else \end{cases} \quad (1)$$

The demand D_i at the retailer i during a period R is a random variable that follows the normal distribution with mean μ_n and standard deviation σ_n. We make the assumption that the demands at the retailers are independent and identically distributed (*i.i.d*).

When this demand causes a stock out during the period of the check at the retailer *1*, then a transshipment will be made from the retailer 2 to 1, the amount of transshipment will be noted by X_{21}. We suppose, too, that the transshipment time is zero and that the unit cost of the transshipment noted C is a linear cost according to the amount transferred between the retailers. Finally, we assume that partial satisfaction of customer demand by the retailer is not allowed and that claims that cannot be satisfied by the available stock and the transshipment are lost and are subject to a cost of break noted C_p per unit lost. In all cases, the available stock becomes zero and will remain zero until the next supply. The mathematical modeling that we study in the following paragraph, concerns a transshipment system composed of two non-identical retailers. The approach we have adopted is inspired from the work of Emel and Lena [21]. Recall that these researchers solved a problem of a stock system (R, S_i) by considering a single central repository and two retailers. Our goal is to begin by identifying the difficulties to be met by the resolution of an inventory system by introducing transshipment in order to identify procedures of resolution for a large number of retailers.

2.1 Constraints

There remain two main constraints in this part of this research work, for the two sites 1 and 2. They are defined as follows:

The stock balance constraint*:*

$$I_1 = PS_{1T} - D_{1T} - X_{12} + X_{21}, \forall R = kT \text{ and } k = 2, 3, 4, \ldots, 10.$$

$$I_2 = PS_{2T} - D_{2T} - X_{21} + X_{12}, \forall R = kT \text{ and } k = 2, 3, 4, \ldots, 10.$$

The constraints of the product transshipment strategy between these two sites:

1. If $D_{1T} < PS_{1T}$ So $X_{21} = X_{12} = 0; \forall R = kT$ and $k = 2, 3, 4, \ldots, 10$.

2. If $D_{2T} < PS_{2T}$ So $X_{21} = X_{12} = 0;$

3. If $D_{1T} \geq PS_{1T}$ So $X_{21} = X_{12} = 0$;

4. If $D_{2T} \geq PS_{2T}$ So $X_{21} = X_{12} = 0$;

5. If $D_{1T} < PS_{1T}$ and $D_{2T} > PS_{2T}$ So $X_{21} = \min\{PS_{1T} - D_{1T}, D_{2T} - PS_{2T}\}$;

6. If $D_{2T} < PS_{2T}$ and $D_{1T} > PS_{1T}$ So $X_{12} = \min\{PS_{2T} - D_{2T}, D_{1T} - PS_{1T}\}$.

From these constraints, we can see that, if the two retailers have excess stocks, then no product transshipment will take place between these depots ($X_{12} = X_{21} = 0$).

Likewise if the two warehouses face a shortage of stock then there will be no collaboration between them ($X_{12} = X_{21} = 0$) and they are forced to place an emergency order from the central warehouse.

But, when depot 1 has a surplus ($I_1 > 0$), while site 2 faces an effective out of stock ($I_2 < 0$), a lateral transfer of product will take place from warehouse 1 to 2 ($X_{12} > 0$) to minimize the Service rate in site 2.

Likewise, when site 2 has excess stock ($I_2 > 0$), while site 1 is facing a failure, a lateral transfer of product from depot 2 to 1 will take place ($X_{21} > 0$) to minimize unfulfilled order quantity for retailer 1.

2.2 Parameters

The notations used in this chapter are as follows:

n: *Number of retailers;*

i: *Retailer index (counter) with i = 1, 2;*

$\boldsymbol{D_{iT}}$: *Demand during the periodicity T at the retailer i (random variable) follows the normal law* (μ_i, σ_i)*.These demands are independent and identically distributed (i. i. d);*

$\boldsymbol{Q_i}$: *The quantity of supply for the retailer i;*

R: *Inventory position revision period, which is divided into k intervals of time of periodicity T;*

$\boldsymbol{S_i}$: *Maximum level of stock at retailer i at the start of the supply cycle;*

$\boldsymbol{PS_{iT}}$: *Stock position at retailer i at each time period T;*

$\overline{\boldsymbol{TDG_i}}$: *Average Global Desservice Rate for i retailers;*

$\overline{\Pi_i^G}(X_G S_i, D_i)$: *Average Global Profit for the two retailers i, with i = 1, 2.*

$\boldsymbol{V_i}$: *Unit selling price for each site i, with i = 1.2.*

$\boldsymbol{C = C_{12} = C_{21}}$: *Unit cost of transshipment whatever the direction of lateral transfer,*

$\boldsymbol{C_{pi}}$: *Unit cost of shortage for such a site i.*

3. Modeling and experimentation

The resolution of our problem is fundamentally based on the probabilistic behavior of customer demands. It is a continuous distribution which follows the normal law.

For this, among the sampling techniques that allow an exploration of customer demand, we selected the simulation. Its principle is then to select, for each demand, random values determined according to an average and a standard deviation. In addition, the demand is generated independently time and between retailers.

We will then, model in this chapter, Two-Retail Stock Distribution System, successively appointed "Without-Transshipment" and "With-Transshipment".

The latter, may be in the form of a transshipment policy called "Complete-Pooling ", if the retailer agrees to transfer all of its available stock if necessary, or by "Partial-Pooling", if the transshipment is carried out by preserving a targeted stock level, by modifying the threshold beyond which the retailer agrees to apply transshipment for each experience. First, the latter will be set at a value which is equal to two times the demand (this is that is to say, to protect the next two demand), then it will be equal, to the next demand and finally it is worth to a safety stock which equals 30% of stock position.

3.1 Case "without-transshipment"

3.1.1 Conceptual model

In this case, if the retailer is confronted with a random demand and to satisfy it and does not fall out of stock, he must demand the missing quantity from the central deposit.

This can be represented by **Figure 1**.

For the Without-Transshipment (***No-Pooling***) case, the modeling by the ARENA 16.0 software can be presented by the **Figure 2**.

3.1.2 Assumptions

To properly model this stock system using the Arena software, it is necessary to list the assumptions and the mode of operation retained in this work:

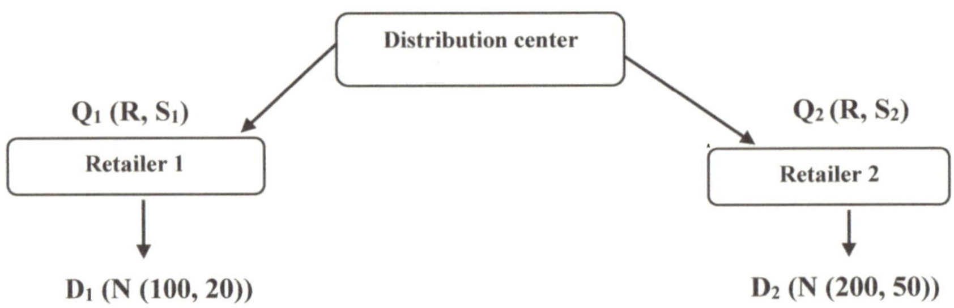

Figure 1.
Two-retailer stock distribution system "without-transshipment".

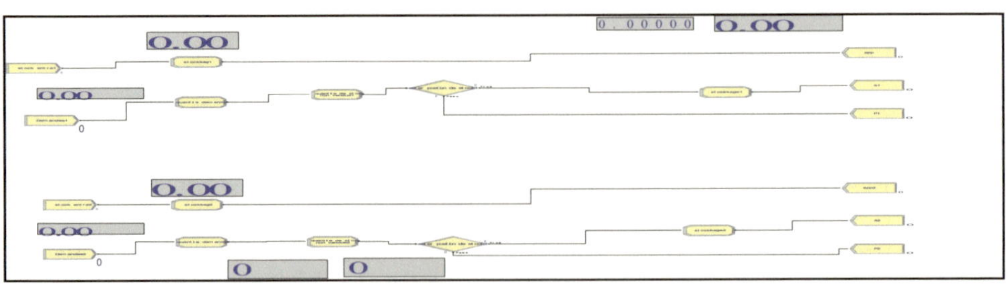

Figure 2.
The simulation model supply chain: no-pooling.

- The storage capacity of the central warehouse is infinite;
- Retailer i applies the storage policy (R, S_i);
- Partial satisfaction of an order is not allowed,
- Any unsatisfied order will be lost;
- Only one order (emergency according to the central depot) is allowed per supply cycle (at the end of period R); with $R = kT$
- There is no definite order of priority. All customer orders are managed according to the same FCFS (First Coming First Served) priority rule;
- The distribution center has sufficient storage capacity, so as not to introduce availability constraints (Unlimited storage policy);
- At the start of each supply cycle, a size order Q_i, (with $Q_i = S_i - PS_{iT}$) is placed to reach the stock level noted S_i.

3.1.3 Mathematical function of average global profit

The Average Global Profit function of our centralized inventory system for two "Without-Transshipment" retailers contains the selling price of the customer product and the cost of the shortage.

It takes the general form of the Eq. 2.

$$\Pi(X_G) = \mathrm{E}\left(\sum_{i=1}^{2} V_i\,(X_i) - C_{pi}\sum_{i=1}^{2}\left(\mathrm{I}_i^-\right)\right). \tag{2}$$

3.2 Case "with-transshipment"

3.2.1 Conceptual model

If one of the two retailers is in the out-of-stock position, then cooperation can be established between them to meet their random demand. This collaboration usually takes the form of "Transshipment-Lateral", also quite simply known as "Transshipment" (**Figure 3**), which allows stocks to be pooled to alleviate the uncertainties relating to demands arriving at sites of the same level.

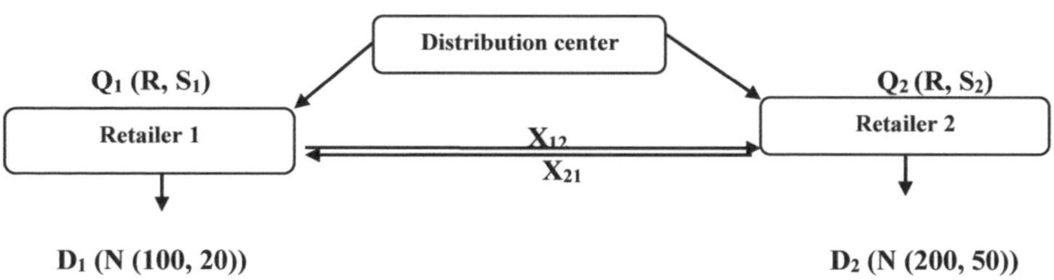

Figure 3.
Two-retail stock distribution system "with-transshipment".

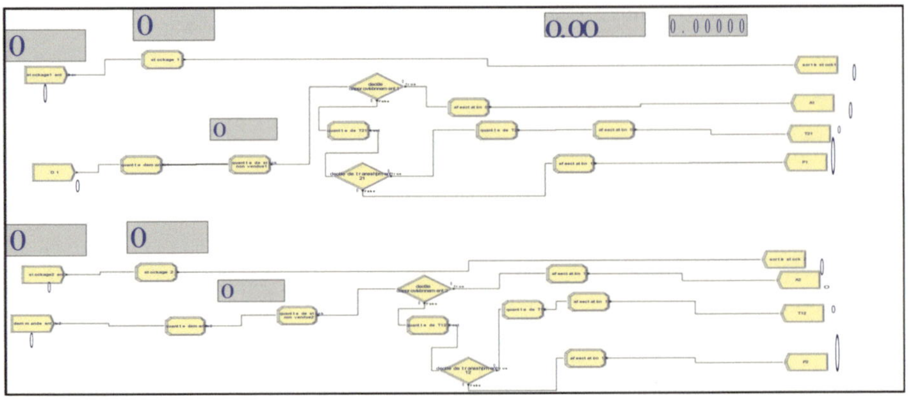

Figure 4.
The simulation model supply chain: complete-pooling.

In this section, we will study two transshipment policies successively named "Complete-Pooling" and "Partial-Pooling".

3.2.2 Transshipment policies

3.2.2.1 "Complete-pooling"

For the first transshipment policy called "Complete-Pooling" the modeling by the ARENA 16.0 software can be presented in **Figure 4**.

3.2.2.2 Assumptions

We consider the following assumptions:

- Retailer 1 confronts a random demand independent of demands from retailer 2;
- The transshipment time is zero;
- In the case where a retailer 1 faces a stock shortage, whereas, the retailer 2 has a surplus of inventory, a transshipment of the necessary quantity (X_{21}) will take place from 2 to 1 to avoid or minimize the shortage: this is the correct transshipment (also called reactive transshipment). Otherwise depot 1 may require an emergency order of size Q_1 at the distribution center;
- In the event of "Complete-Pooling", the retailer who is in the overstock position agrees to transfer all of his available stock if necessary.

3.2.2.3 Mathematical function of average global profit

The function of Average Global Profit for our centralized system composed of two levels and two retailers, by integrating transshipment and applying the "Complete-Pooling" policy, can be formulated by the Eq. 3.

$$\overline{\Pi}(X_G) = E\left(V_1\,(X_1 + X_{21}) + V_2\,(X_2 + X_{12}) - C\,(X_{12} + X_{21}) - C_{pi}\left(\sum_{i=1}^{2} I_i^-\right)\right) \quad (3)$$

With $X_G = X_1 + X_2 + X_{12} + X_{21}$

3.2.2.4 Quantity of transhipment

We assume that retailer 1 is the one facing a stock shortage, so according to this transshipment policy, retailer 2 agrees to transfer all of its available stock if necessary, even if this stock is not enough to fill any the demand of the client who is at the origin of the demand for the transshipment. The quantity of the transshipment, according to this policy, will be formulated in the form of the Eq. (4).

$$X_{21} = \begin{cases} D_{1T} - PS_{1T} & if\, D_{1T} - PS_{1T} \leq PS_{2T} \\ 0 & Else \end{cases} \quad (4)$$

3.2.2.5 Objective function

The objective is to identify the most economically profitable transshipment policy for a centralized system over a finite time horizon R, by seeking the lowest possible Average Global Desservice Rate.

For this, the objective function of the "Complete-Pooling" transshipment policy will be defined in the form of the Eq. (5).

$$\text{Max}\ (E\left(V1(X_1 + X_{21}) + V2(X_2 + X_{12}) - C\,(X_{12} + X_{21}) - C_{pi}\left(\sum_{i=1}^{2} I_i^-\right)\right).$$

S/C

$$X_{12}\sum_{i\neq j} X_{ij} \leq PS_{1T},\ \text{With } T = R/k \text{ et } k = 2, 3, 4, \ldots, 10. \quad (5)$$

$$X_{21}\sum_{i\neq j} X_{ij} \leq PS_{2T}\ \text{With } T = R/k \text{ et } k = 2, 3, 4, \ldots, 10.$$

$$S_i \geq 1 \text{ Strictly positive integer}, \forall i = 1, 2$$

With

$S_i = \left(\mu_i * k + \sigma_i\sqrt{k}\right), \forall i = 1, 2$ and k:being the number of periodicities, with $k = 2, 3, 4, \ldots, 10$.

And $X_i \sim N\ (\mu_i, \sigma_i)$.

3.2.2.6 "Partial-pooling"

For the second transshipment policy called "Partial-Pooling" the modeling by the ARENA 16.0 software can be presented in **Figure 5**.

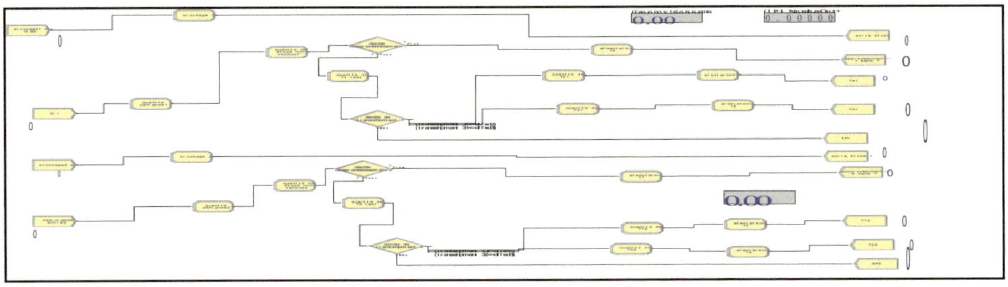

Figure 5.
The simulation model supply chain: partial-pooling.

3.2.2.7 Assumptions

Furthermore, the hypotheses already indicated for the "Complete-Pooling" transshipment policy, we can add another specific assumption for the "Partial-Pooling" policy, that is, the lateral transfer is carried out while preserving a level of targeted stock. We find in research work the following variants:

- The retailer accepts the transshipment up to the amount of surplus stock to its safety stock,
- the retailer accepts the transshipment up to the amount of surplus stock at his order point,
- the retailer accepts the transshipment up to the amount of surplus stock at the estimated demand for the following period (See, Archibald et al. [7]).
- the decision to make a transshipment at the level of a retailer depends on the current stock level and the time remaining before the next supply.

In our chapter, we are interested in the third variant where the retailer accepts the transshipment up to the amount of surplus demand for a first proposal of the threshold value. Then we add two other personal contributions, first estimating that it will be equal to "Two multiply by demand". Secondly, it will be equal to "30% of stock position", to improve the Average Global Profit of the entire system made up of two retailers while minimizing as far as possible the average stock-out (Average Global Desservice Rate).

In the following sections of this chapter, we first describe the mathematical modeling of a "Without-Transshipment" stock system for a warehouse number set to two. Then we modify it, by integrating, the two policies of transshipment, named, successively, "Complete-Pooling" and "Partial-Pooling".

3.2.2.8 Mathematical function of average global profit

The function of the average global profit apply the transshipment policy "Partial-Pooling", requires the integration of the quantity lost for each retailer after the accumulation of stock.

The average global profit function will be formulated by the Eq. (6).

$$\overline{\Pi}(X_G) = (E\ (V_1(X_1 + X_{21}) + V_2(X_2 + X_{12}) - C\ (X_{12} + X_{21}) - C_{pi}\left(\sum_{i=1}^{2} I_i^- + X_{P1} + X_{P2}\right) \tag{6}$$

With $X_G = X_1 + X_2 + X_{12} + X_{21}$

And X_{P1} : The quantity lost for retailer 1 after the accumulation of stock with partial transshipment.

X_{P2} : The quantity lost for retailer 2 after the accumulation of stock with partial transshipment.

3.2.2.9 Quantity of transhipment

To significantly improve a purely reactive transshipment policy, it would be possible to combine it with another proactive policy; this will be named by "Hybrid transshipment policy".

In this area of research, the policy of transshipment "Partial-Pooling", to put the action on the importance of the estimate of the future to minimize as soon as possible the quantity not satisfied which governs positively on the economic profitability.

We estimate that retailer 1 is facing an actual stock shortage, therefore, the amount of lateral transfer from retailer 2 to 1 to minimize or avoid this lost quantity, according to this transshipment policy will be carried out while preserving a targeted stock level. Named the transshipment threshold and it will be formulated by three equations according to the fixing of the latter.

First of all, we estimate that it will be worth to Twice multiply by the Demand, for this, the quantity of transshipment from 2 to 1 will be formulated by the Eq. (7).

$$\begin{cases} \text{If } (PS_{2T} - 2 * D_{2T}) > 0 & \begin{cases} \text{If } (D_{1T} - PS_{1T}) \leq (PS_{2T} - 2 * D_{2T}) \text{ So } X_{21} = D_{1T} - PS_{1T} \\ \text{Else } X_{P1} = (PS_{2T} - 2 * D_{2T}) \text{ Lost order} \end{cases} \\ \text{Else order lost} \end{cases} \tag{7}$$

Then we assume that this threshold is equal to the Next Demand, and then the amount of lateral transfer from 2 to 1 will be formulated by the Eq. (8).

$$\begin{cases} \text{If } (PS_{2T} - D_{2T}) > 0 & \begin{cases} \text{If } (D_{1T} - PS_{1T}) \leq (PS_{2T} - D_{2T}) \text{ So } X_{21} = D_{1T} - PS_{1T} \\ \text{Else } X_{P1} = (PS_{2T} - D_{2T}) \text{ Lost order} \end{cases} \\ \text{Else order lost} \end{cases} \tag{8}$$

Finally, we propose that it be equal to a safety stock which is worth 30% of $\boldsymbol{PS_{iT}}$, therefore, the amount of transshipment will be formulated by the Eq. (9).

$$\begin{cases} \text{If } (PS_{2T} - 30\% * PS_{2T}) > 0 & \begin{cases} \text{If } (D_{1T} - PS_{1T}) \leq (PS_{2T} - 30\% * PS_{2T}) \text{ So } X_{21} = D_{1T} - PS_{1T} \\ \text{Else } X_{P1} = (PS_{2T} - 30\% * PS_{2T}) \text{ Lost order} \end{cases} \\ \text{Else order lost} \end{cases} \tag{9}$$

3.2.2.10 Objective function

For the second transshipment policy ("Partial-Pooling"), the objective function will be defined in the form of the Eq. (10).

$$\text{Max}\left(\text{E}\left(\text{V}_1(X_1+X_{21})+\text{V}_2(X_2+X_{12})-\text{C}\,(X_{12}+X_{21})-C_{pi}\left(\sum_{i=1}^{2}I_i^-+X_{P1}+X_{P2}\right)\right)\right) \tag{10}$$

$(PS_{2T}-\text{Threshold}_{2T})>0$

$(PS_{1T}-\text{Threshold}_{1T})>0$

With $Threshold_{iT}$= Twice the Demand, Next Demand and 30% of PS_{iT}

And X_{P1} : The quantity lost for retailer 1 after the accumulation of stock with partial transshipment.

And X_{P2} : The quantity lost for retailer 2 after the accumulation of stock with partial transshipment.

With $\text{T}=\text{R}/\text{k}$ et $\text{k}=2,3,4,\ \dots,10$.

$S_i \geq 1$ Strictly positive integer, $\forall i$ = *1, 2*

With

$S_i=\left(\mu_i*\text{k}+\sigma_i\sqrt{\text{k}}\right),\forall i=1,2$ and k:being the number of periodicities, With k = 2, 3, 4, ... ,10.

And $X_i \sim N\ (\mu_i, \sigma_i)$.

4. Simulation results

We recall that, according to Meissner and Rusyaeva [22], the initial level of replenishment for a demand that follows the normal law of mean and standard deviation, will take the form of the equation and will be calculated by applying the Eq. 11.

$$S_n^0=\left(\mu_n*\text{T}+\sigma_n\sqrt{\text{T}}\right) \tag{11}$$

With:

T: number of periods

μ_i :average demand during the period *T* of retailer *i*, with *i* = 1, 2.

σ_i :standard deviation of demand of retailer *i*, with *i* = 1, 2.

Table 1 shows the different measures of initial stock level of replication and for n = 2, with N: number of retailers.

Recall that the network structure considered in this chapter is made up of a distribution center and two retailers, who face random and non-identical demands on average and standard deviation. We assume that the simulation length is 10 years.

We have assumed that the demandD_1 of the first retailer follows the law N (100, 20) and that of the second retailer, D_2 follows the law N (200, 50). These demands are Independent and identically distributed *(i.i.d)*.

Also, we have considered in all the examples of our research that:

- The revision period R = 28 days, (Based on Emel and Lena, [21]);

k	S_1^0	S_2^0
2	229	470
3	335	687
4	440	900
5	545	1112
6	648	1322
7	753	1532
8	857	1741
9	960	1950
10	1063	2158

Table 1.
Determination of different measures of the initial level of replenishment.

- The unit sale price for retailer 1 equal to 95 $ and that of retailer 2 is worth 125 $,
- The unit cost of rupture whatever the site is equal to 30 $,
- The unit cost of transshipment =3 $, 0.5 $, k = 2, 3, 4, ... , 10.

We led to the resolution of our problem via simulation by successively testing the "Without transshipment" and "With-transshipment" policies. We then give the following performance measures, for the evaluation of the contribution to perform the Pooling between the retailers:

- The number of supply orders (without transshipment),
- The number of orders received with the transshipment application,
- The amount of lateral transfer from a warehouse which is in overstock position to that of the same level which is in rupture position,
- The quantity of order not fulfilled at a retailer (quantity lost),
- Average Global Profit at a retailer,
- The Average Desservice Rate (the rate of customer dissatisfaction after the transshipment).

In **Table 1** we present the different measures of the initial stock level of the replenishment.

4.1 Impact of input parameters on average global profit

We examine the effect of three input parameters on the benefits of transshipment, namely:

- The periodicity "T",
- The unit cost of transshipment,
- And, the threshold of the "Partial-Pooling" transshipment policy.

4.1.1 Impact of the periodicity "T"

4.1.1.1 "Without-transshipment" system vs. "With-transshipment" system

The numbers calculated in **Table 1** reveal the considerable effect of collaboration between the sites in terms of Average Global Profit.

Likewise, they present the results of the performance evaluation of the "Complete-Pooling" and "Partial-Pooling" transshipment policies compared to the "Without-Transshipment" policy. We note, first, that these results verify those already obtained by the mathematical model for a stock system with two non-identical retailers, namely that:

- the comparative values obtained by simulation in **Table 1**, using the "ARENA" software, confirm the evidence of the advantage of the application of "transshipment" between the sites in terms of improving the Average Global Profit. For example, for k = 2, "Complete-Pooling" improved the performance of the centralized inventory system by increasing the average value of Average Profit Global of the two retailers, from 39,125 to 44,087, that is to say, a relative change worth 13%,
- These values show the effect of the change in periodicity on economic profitability, by improving the Average Global Profit from k = 2 to k = 4. Whereas, the evolution of the value of the latter undergoes an imperfection beyond k = 4, and this will be explicit for k = 5 up to k = 10,

because, in these periodicities, this profit becomes under the shape of a decreasing curve because of the increase in the number of customer orders by the period R = 28 days.

4.1.1.2 "Complete-pooling" vs. "partial-pooling"

Comparative Average Global Profit Improvement Percentage Values Obtained by Simulation Using ARENA Software for the Two Transshipment Policies "Complete-Pooling" and "Partial-Pooling" are reported in **Table 2**.

K	Without-transshipment/ complete-pooling	Complete-pooling/partial-pooling: *Twice the Demand*	Complete-pooling/partial-pooling: *next demand*	Complete-pooling/partial-pooling: *security stock = 30% of* PS_{iT}
2	13%	3%	17%	26%
3	15%	2%	14%	18%
4	16%	1%	8%	11%

Table 2.
Determination of the values of the relative improvement percentage of the average global profit for a unit cost of transshipment = 3 $.

To calculate the different percentages of relative improvement in Average Global Profit indicated in **Table 2**, we apply the mathematical formula (12).

$$\Big[\%\text{of Relative improvement} = \overline{\Pi_i^G}(\text{complete} - \text{pooling}) - \overline{\Pi_i^G}(\text{without} - \text{transshipment}) \\ /\overline{\Pi_i^G}(\text{without} - \text{transshipment})) * 100\Big] \tag{12}$$

(This for the first column of the table while for the two transshipment policies ("Complete-Pooling" and "Partial-Pooling") we apply this formula while looking for the percentage improvement value between them).

From **Table 2**, we see that, the percentage improvement in Average Global Profit, depends on the periodicity T, as well as, on the transshipment policy applied, ("Complete-Pooling" or "Partial-Pooling").

We note that the first lateral transfer policy ("Complete-Pooling") improves the economic profitability of the "No-transshipment" policy but with a percentage of improvement less than that of the transshipment policy ("Partial- Pooling"). Because of this, the latter is more advantageous, because the Average Global Profit of the former will be improved regardless of the threshold applied. We will conclude, too, that the modification of the latter acts on this improvement, take as an example, for k = 2, the "Partial-Pooling" with a threshold of the "Twice the Demand" target to reach a percentage of improvement Relative Average Global Profit of "Complete-Pooling" equal to 3% but with the change of the threshold to "Next Demand" this value is worth 17% and finally for a threshold equal to "SS = 30% of PS_{iT}" and becomes equal to 26%. By analyzing the variation of the threshold of the "Partial-Pooling" transshipment policy, we note that if the latter is higher than this leads to reducing the chances of supply which results in an increase in the demand no satisfaction rate.

This allows us to conclude that the most economically profitable transshipment policy is that of "Partial-Pooling" and especially with a lateral transfer threshold equal to "SS = 30% of PS_{iT}". This observation leads to a first conclusion in our research, namely that the change of the threshold influences the percentage improvement relative to the Average Global Profit.

4.1.2 Impact of the unit cost of transshipment and the threshold for transshipment

The study of the impact of the variation in the unit cost of transshipment on the Average Global Profit is carried out in cases where C = 0.5 $. The simulation results are presented in **Table 3**.

4.1.2.1 "Without-transshipment" system vs. "with-transshipment" system

We examine, for a stock system composed of two levels and two non-identical retailers, the impact of the variation in the unit cost of transshipment and the threshold of the "Partial-Pooling" policy.

The results of the simulation presented in **Table 3** show that a variation in this unit cost of transshipment, by reducing it from 3$ to 0.5$, acts mainly on improving the profitability of the entire centralized system between the "Without -Transshipment "and that of "With-Transshipment", for that, we will conclude that, the coordination between the sites of the same level allows to improve the profitability of the whole system, but it reaches the

K	Without-transshipment	Complete-pooling	Partial-pooling		
			Twice the demand	Next demandS	Security stock = 30% of PS_{iT}
2	39,125	45,054	46,938	52,502	56,400
3	65,044	75,754	77,740	85,952	88,976
4	88,000	102,306	103,510	110,200	113,800
5	86,240	101,200	102,520	105,035	107,097
6	83,600	97,657	99,125	101,257	103,356
7	80,960	94,230	95,127	96,102	98,235
8	78,320	91,560	93,276	94,605	97,203
9	70,400	82,359	83,900	88,007	90,102
10	66,000	77,135	79,230	84,009	87,990

Table 3.
Determination of the average global profit for a unit cost of transshipment = 0.5 $.

most effective values by the application of the "Partial-Pooling" transshipment policy and above all with the fixing of the threshold at "security stock = 30% of PS_{iT}".

For this, we will first of all look for the relative improvement percentage of the Average Global Profit of the centralized system for the first "Complete-Pooling" transshipment policy by reducing this cost (see **Table 4**), then by calculating it with the integration of the second "Partial-Pooling" policy (see **Table 5**).

4.1.2.2 "Complete-pooling" vs. "partial-pooling"

The determination of the various relative improvement percentage values of the Average Global Profit for the "Complete-Pooling" transshipment policy or (simply noted CP) between C = 3 $ and C = 0.5 $, is done by applying the Eq. 13.

K	Percentage improvement in average global profit
2	2%
3	2%
4	1%

Table 4.
Determination of the percentage improvement in average global profit for "complete pooling" between C = 3 $ and C = 0.5$.

k	Pourcentage du Profit Global Moyen		
	Twice the demand	Next demands	Security stock = 30% of PS_{iT}
2	3%	2%	2%
3	1%	1%	1%
4	1%	3%	2%

Table 5.
Determination of the percentage improvement in average global profit for partial pooling between C = 3$ and C = 0.5$.

$$\left(\left[\overleftarrow{\boldsymbol{\Pi}}_{\mathrm{i}\ (\mathrm{CP\ for\ C=0.5\$})}^{\boldsymbol{G}}\right]-\left[\overleftarrow{\boldsymbol{\Pi}}_{\mathrm{i}\ (\mathrm{CP\ for\ C=3\$})}^{\boldsymbol{G}}\right]/\left[\overleftarrow{\boldsymbol{\Pi}}_{\mathrm{i}\ (\mathrm{CP\ for\ C=3\$})}^{\boldsymbol{G}}\right]*100\right) \tag{13}$$

According to the **Table 4**, we quote for example that, for k = 3 and with a unit cost of transshipment equal to 3$, the "Complete-Pooling" transshipment policy improved the value of average overall profit "Without-Transshipment" from 65,044 to 74,538, therefore with an improvement value equal to 15%.

But, with a slight reduction in the unit cost of transshipment, this percentage becomes equal to 17%. For this, we will conclude that the unit cost of transshipment has an influence on the improvement of the Average Global Profit of the whole centralized stock system.

From **Table 5**, we will conclude that the application of the unit cost of transshipment equal to 1 $ is more profitable in terms of gain compared to that which is worth 2 $, and this is remarkable from the results presented in this table, but with a small percentage of improvement.

For example,

- For a threshold = Twice the Demand: the "Partial-Pooling" transshipment policy with a unit cost equal to 0.5 $ makes it possible to improve the Average Global Profit of the one that equals 3 $ with a minimum value equal to 1% up to a maximum value equal to 3%.

- For a threshold = Next Demand: With a unit cost of transshipment worth $ 0.5, the "Partial-Pooling" transshipment policy has improved the Average Global Profit by that which equals 3 $ with a minimum value equal to 1% up to a maximum value equal to 3%.

- For a threshold = 30% of PS_{iT}: With a unit cost of transshipment equal to 0.5$, the economic profitability of the centralized system for the policy of transshipment "Partial-Pooling" undergoes an evolution compared to that which equals 3 $ of a minimum value equal to 1% up to a maximum value equal to 2%.

In fact, according to the study of the impact of the change in the unit cost of transshipment and the threshold of the "Partial-Pooling" policy on the improvement of Average Global Profit, the analysis of the sensitivity of performance to this variation can be summarized as follows:

- The decrease in the unit cost of transshipment influences the increase in the percentage of relative improvement in economic profitability.

- The evolution of Average Global Profit has a strong relationship with the modification of the threshold beyond which the retailer accepts the transshipment to design of available stock.

4.2 Impact of the input parameters on the average global deservice rate (the "T" periodicity and the transshipment threshold)

We focus here on determining, the policy of transshipment in a centralized stock system which seeks to improve the Average Global Profit at the two retailers by minimizing the Average Global Desservice Rate as much as possible.

In this section of chapter, we formulate the Average Global Desservice Rate for the two retailers by Eq. (14).

$$\overline{\mathbf{TDG}}_{\mathrm{i}} = \boldsymbol{E}\left(\sum_{i=1}^{2}\left(\mathbf{I}_{\mathrm{i}}^{-}/\mathbf{D}_{\mathrm{i}}\right)\right), \tag{14}$$

(this is the Average Global Desservice Rate).

From the analysis in **Table 6**, we note that the Average Global Desservice Rate has a strong relationship with the change in periodicity and it increases beyond k = 4, and becomes in the form of a increasing curve.

But, we analyze the effect of transshipment policies on the minimization of the Average Global Desservice Rate. We notice then that, the first transshipment policy "Complete-Pooling" aims to decrease the rate of the quantity of customer orders not satisfied whatever the periodicity and for example for k = 2 this reduction is worth from 0.500 to 0.360 and that the second "Partial-Pooling" policy aims to reduce it as soon as possible and this will be explicit for the last transshipment threshold which equals ***Security Stock = 30% of*** $\boldsymbol{PS_{iT}}$.

We then note that the collaboration between two sites 1 and 2 increases the probability of cycles without shortages in each warehouse by the quantity of transshipment transferred planned from 2 to 1 and likewise from 1 to 2 for an increase in the quantity to order for the site 1 and for site 2. Which results in the probability of customer satisfaction improves after the application of the transshipment.

We will then conclude that, the level of service in a collaborative network is higher compared to the network of independent sites and this plays a very important role in decreasing the amount of lost order. This implies that the economic performance of the group of employees does not only depend on the characteristics of each isolated site, it also depends on the characteristics of each retailer and its relationship with the other depots that make up the inventory system and especially when the cost of transfer lateral is weak. This conclusion should be taken into account in the training of employee groups.

k	Without-transshipment	Complete-pooling	Partial-pooling		
			Twice the demand	Next demandS	Security Stock = 30% of PS_{iT}
2	0.500	0.360	0.340	0.120	0.060
3	0.600	0.460	0.432	0.097	0.050
4	0.450	0.159	0.148	0.053	0.032
5	0.670	0.357	0.351	0.157	0.067
6	0.750	0.465	0.457	0.195	0.090
7	0.865	0.525	0.512	0.293	0.120
8	0.925	0.620	0.602	0.387	0.202
9	1.005	0.770	0.720	0.492	0.297
10	1.121	0.800	0.795	0.537	0.325

Table 6.
Determination of average global desservice rate.

5. Conclusions and perspectives

This chapter targets to study the effect of collaboration in emergencies and applying two policy of transshipment named, "Complete-Pooling" and "Partial-Pooling" between two storage sites on the overall average profit of the system centralized and customer Desservice level.

The most important conclusions can be summarized in the following:

- The sharing of stocks between sites of the same level greatly optimizes the Average Global Profit of the entire system;
- Collaboration between sites always improves customer Average Global Desservice Rate, i.e. the probability of no-shortage cycles and the probability of customer satisfaction;
- In general, the positive effect of collaboration is greater when we apply the "partial pooling" policy with a change in the transshipment threshold.

Several extensions of this model that are of particular interest can be considered in future research. For example, the variation in the average and the standard deviation of the random customer demand and the use of the larger network where the number of sites exceeds the two, integrating the distance between the different storage sites located at the same level.

Author details

Elleuch Fadoi
Faculty of Economics and Management of Sfax, Sfax, Tunisia

*Address all correspondence to: elleuchfadoi@gmail.com

References

[1] Derhami S, Montreuil B, Baua G. Assessing product availability in omni channel retail networks in the presence of on-demand inventory transshipment and product substitution. Omega. 2020; **102**(2):1-14

[2] Wong H, Cattrysse D, Van Oudheusden D. Inventory pooling of repairable spare parts with non-zero lateral transshipment time and delayed lateral transshipments. European Journal of Operational Research. Elsevier. 2005; **165**(1):207-218

[3] Herer YT, Tzur M, Yücesan E. Transshipment: An emerging inventory recourse to achieve supply chain legality. International Journal of Production Economics. 2002;**80**(3):201-212

[4] Paterson C, Teunter R, Glazebrook K. Enhanced lateral transshipments in a multi-location inventory system. European Journal of Operational Research. 2012;**221**(2):317-332

[5] Noham R, Tzur M. The single and multi-item transshipment problem with fixed transshipment costs. Naval Research Logistics. 2014;**61**(8):637-664

[6] Van G, Houtum J, Zijm WHM. On the relation between cost and service models for general inventory systems. Statistica Neerlandica. 2009;**54**:127-147

[7] Archibald TW, Blacka D, Glazebrook KD. An index heuristic for transhipment decisions in multi-location inventory systems based on a pairwise decomposition. European Journal of Operational Research. 2009;**192**(1):69-78

[8] Li X, Sun L, Gao J. Coordinating preventive lateral transshipment between two locations. Computers & Industrial Engineering. 2013;**66**(4):933-943

[9] Liao Y, Shen W, Hu X, Yang S. Optimal responses to stockouts: Lateral transshipment versus emergency order policies. Omega. 2014;**49**(12):79-92

[10] Olsson F. Emergency lateral transshipments in a two-location inventory system with positive transshipment leadtimes. European Journal of Operational Research. 2015; **242**(2):424-433

[11] Torabi S, Hassini E, Jeihoonian M. Fulfillment source allocation, inventory transshipment, and customer order transfer in e-tailing. Transportation Research Part E: Logistics and Transportation Review. 2015;**79**:128-144

[12] Lee C, Park KS. Inventory and transshipment decisions in the rationing game under capacity uncertainty. Omega. 2016;**65**:82-97

[13] Feng X, Moon I, Ryu K. Warehouse capacity sharing via transshipment for anintegrated two-echelon supply chain. Transportation Research Part E. Logistics and Transportation Review. 2017;**104**:17-35

[14] Silbermayr L, Jammernegg W, Kischka P. Inventory pooling with environmental constraints using copulas. European Journal of Operational Research. 2017;**263**(2)

[15] Nakandala D, Lau H, Shum PKC. A lateral transshipment model for perishable inventory management. International Journal of Production Research. 2017;**1**:n1-n14

[16] Timajchi A, Al-E-Hashem SMJM, Rekik Y. Inventory routing problem for hazardous and deteriorating items in the presence of accident risk with

transhipment option. International Journal of Production Economics. 2018; **209**:302-315

[17] Feng P, Feng W, Richard FY. Evaluation of two transshipment policies in a two-location decentralized inventory system under partial backordering. Transportation Research Part E: Logistics and Transportation Review. 2018;**118**:207-224

[18] Dehghani M, Abbasi B. An age-based lateral-transshipment policy for perishable items. International Journal of Production Economics. 2018;**198**:93-103

[19] Timajchi A, Seyed MJ, Al-e-Hashem M, Rekik Y. Inventory routing problem for hazardous and deteriorating items in the presence of accident risk with transshipment option. International Journal of Production Economics. 2019; **209**:302-315

[20] Liao Y, Li J, Hu X, Li Y, Shen W. Application of lateral transshipment in cost reduction of decentralized systems. Sustainability. 2020;**12**:1-20

[21] Emel A, Lena S. Risk pooling via unidirectional inventory transshipments in a decentralized supply chain. International Journal of Production Research. 2017

[22] Meissner J, Rusyaeva O. Approximate dynamic programming for lateral transshipment problems. European Journal of Operational Research. 2016;**265**

Chapter 7

New Product Development Strategies and Methods: Implications for the Indian Readymade Apparel Sector

Mitali Gupta

Abstract

Today, the intense global competition in the textile and apparel industry made the firms worldwide to be more innovative and competitive by heavily investing into the New Product Development Strategies and Methods. In this context, the present study attempts to (i) understand New Product Development Approaches and Strategies adopted by key global and domestic brands operating in the Indian market and (ii) derive lessons for the development of future models of New Product Development in the Indian Textile and Apparel Industry. The brands have been selected on the basis of their popularity and positioning in the Indian Textile markets.

Keywords: product innovation, design, textile industry, India, new product development

1. Introduction

Today, the global competition in the textile and apparel industry has become more intense due to the changes in the global lifestyle trends and patterns and increased per capita consumption over the last few decades. To compete in the future, the firms worldwide are immensely resorting to be innovative while reducing cycle times and cutting costs which can be achieved by heavily investing in the New Product Development Strategies and Methods, which has been termed as one of the 'riskiest' and 'most important' endeavours of the modern corporation [1]. In fact, today, the role and importance of innovation is seen to be more significant towards achieving sustainable development and social welfare than economic growth alone of a firm/ country pair [2–9].

The Global Apparel market is close to 2.3% of world GDP with Europe, USA and China being the largest markets. However, the year 2020–2021 witnessed a lot of changes in the Global Apparel Industry owing to the Covid-19 pandemic which has largely impacted the domestic and overseas apparel markets of India as well. As, the pandemic forced people to stay at home, the online apparel sales surged during the last 2 years, prompting many brands to offer their unique product lines through fast-track digitization and e-commerce platforms leading largely to the occurrence of supply side innovations. Since the apparel business is considered to be one of the most challenging businesses as factors such as short product life cycle, volatile fashions, unpredictable market trends and impulse purchase nature of the customer are the ones which drive the sector's demand at large, keeping up pace with such factors in these times of uncertainties would be an additional challenge to be addressed by both the national and multi-national apparel brands operating in India along with the strategic management of their core organisation policies.

The Indian Textile Industry, one of the oldest manufacturing sectors in the country, has been known for its overwhelming presence in the economic life of the country while playing a pivotal role through its contribution to the total industrial output (14% to industrial production and 4% to the GDP), employment generation (direct employment to about 35 million people which includes a substantial number of SC/ ST and women population) and the total export earnings (17% share). Endowed with the largest loom age in the world, the second highest spindle age (accounting for 24% of the world's spindle capacity next only to China), a strong multi-fibre raw material base, a vast pool of skilled workers, flexible production systems, a dynamic entrepreneurship together with vibrant design creativity, the Indian Textile Industry has been growing at a CAGR of 10.23% and is as diverse and complex as the country itself. India is the second largest producer of textiles and garments and sixth largest exporter of textiles spanning apparel, home and technical products in the world. According to the data from McKinsey's Fashion Scope, India's clothing and garment market is forecast to be worth over $59.3 billion in 2022.

However, it is to be noted that despite its substantial contribution, the share of investment in R&D per capita is very low in the Indian Textile industry as compared to the other developed countries. The industry is largely decentralised in nature wherein only 4%–5% of the total cloth production comes from the organised sector. The absence of innovation in Product Design in the Indian Textile Industry is a major policy concern where, in the globalised competitive market, product innovation has become essential for catering to consumer's ever-changing preferences. Design thinking is now considered essential to product development and the policy implementation depends substantially on the design of products and services. In this context, it is understood that it would be difficult to sustain this sector's growth and exports unless enterprises are enabled with a pro-active approach towards product innovation and development. Also, there are a very few focussed studies on various approaches and strategies adopted by the Indian companies and the multi-national apparel brands operating in India and their performance owing to adoption of such strategies thus providing an apt rationale for undertaking the present study in an extensive manner.

2. Concept of product innovation

A Product Innovation is the introduction of a good or service that is altogether 'New' or has significantly improved characteristics or intended uses. According to the Green Paper released by the European Commission (1995:6), Innovation can be defined as, "The competitiveness of a country, region or firm now depends predominantly on its capacity to invest in research, know-how, technology and the skills which allow maximum benefit to be derived from these in terms of new products or services" [10] (European Commission, 1995: 6). On a similar note, [3, 11, 12] define innovation as "the generation and implementation of new or improved processes, products/services, production methods or single actions aimed at increasing the competitiveness of an enterprise". Extending this definition, [3, 12] have defined innovation as "the successful exploitation of a new product, service, process, organization or a new business model which is new to a company, new to a market or new to the world".

Schumpeter [13] originally classified innovations into five types: new products; new processes (technological process innovation and organisational innovation); new sources of supply/raw materials; new markets and new ways organisation. Gradually, OECD Innovation Manual and other such studies identified four main types of innovation based on the object of change and these are product, process, marketing and organisational innovations [3]. Further according to [14], any new product development undergoes eight stages before it is finally launched in the market. These are: (i) generation of new product ideas, (ii) screening and evaluation of ideas, (iii) concept development and testing, (iv) marketing strategy, (v) business analysis, (vi) product development, (vii) test marketing and (viii) commercialisation.

3. Methodology

3.1 Objectives and hypothesis of the study

Based on the above discussion, the present study has the following objectives:

i. To examine various approaches and strategies of product innovation undertaken by various national and multi-national brands operating in India to remain competitive in the domestic and overseas markets. It is hypothesised that the major proportion of development of New Product categories is being undertaken in the category of 'New Product Lines' followed by the 'Addition to the Product Lines' involved in the process of developing a new product in the Indian Textile Industry.

ii. To provide future policy perspectives on the models of product development strategies to enhance global competitiveness of the Indian Readymade Apparel Companies.

3.2 Methodology of the study

To understand the nature and various dimensions of product innovation in the Textile industry the present study follows the classification made by [1, 15, 16] in their respective papers wherein they have identified the following types of new product categories:

i. New-to-the world products

According to [15], these are the products which revolutionise existing product categories or define wholly the 'new' ones based on the ever-changing and innovative technologies. Cooper [1] identifies such products as the first of their kind and create altogether a new market and customer base. This category represents a very small share of the overall products present in the market.

ii. New product lines

These are those products which are not new to the world but place a firm into a new product line and thus diversify the product portfolio of the company. Studies have shown that they constitute a substantial share of the overall new product launches in the market.

iii. Additions to the product lines/product improvements

These products constitute line extensions which fit within an existing product line that the firm already produces with an aim to improve/modify the quality or standards of an existing product range. They may also provide enhanced performance or greater perceived value over the existing range of products. According to [1, 16], this category constitutes one of the largest share of overall categories of the New Product Development in the market. This process is basically about differentiating products to gain edge over the competitor's products and usually practiced by small business firms which are constrained by their resources to create an altogether a new product.

iv. Repositioning products for a newer application or customer base

Repositioning has been identified as a new application for the existing products, solving a new problem and or serving the new customer base.

v. Cost reductions strategies

These are those products which are designed to replace existing products at a lower cost while offering similar benefits and performance. These are also considered to be the dominant strategies for capturing a given market or customer base.

The present study attempts to include and capture various dimensions of the above product categories in detail by presenting the case of 12 national and multinational apparel brands operating in India. The study has been conducted by undertaking rigorous desk research and in-depth interviews of the professionals constituting the core team responsible for undertaking R&D activities in a given company. The selection of the brands is based largely on the share of market penetration and popularity of a brand in a particular category of clothing.

4. New product development in the textile and apparel industry in India

The Readymade Garment Sector of India is largely comprised of three main types of clothing: (i) formal wear, (ii) casual wear (which largely includes sports-wear and active wear also and to an extent innerwear/sleepwear as well) and (iii) traditional or ethnic wear. We discuss product development strategies separately under each of the above mentioned categories.

4.1 Formal clothing

Some of the major players in this segment in the Indian market are Raymond, Siyaram's and Van Heusen and their product development strategies are shown in **Table 1** below.

Strategy of product innovation	Raymond	Siyarams'	Van Heusen
New-to-the-world products	✓		✓
New product lines	✓	✓	✓
Additions to the product Lines/product improvement			
Repositioning	✓		✓
Cost reductions			

Source: Author's own assessment of the Product Portfolio of the Apparel brands.

Table 1.
Strategies of new product development in the Indian formal clothing segment.

4.1.1 The Raymond group

The Raymond Group, established in 1925, constitutes one of the most respected and largest apparel manufacturers in the country reckoned for delivering world class fabrics to its customers from the past nine decades. The company has 60% market share in the overall Indian Suiting business which amounts to a total of Rs. 18,000 crores and today has become the largest exporter of men's suits in the world. It operates through a vast network of 700 stores and 200+ cities in India and worldwide and is one of the largest horizontally and vertically integrated worsted suiting manufacturer in the world. It has its headquarters in Mumbai, Maharashtra and owns many production facilities in the overseas markets as well. The well-known brands under this company are Park Avenue, Raymond Premium Apparel, Parx, Colour Plus and Ethnix. The state of the art and wholly owned subsidiaries of the Raymond Group such as Silver Spark Apparel Ltd., Celebrations Apparel Ltd. and Ever Blue Apparel Ltd. produce crafts suits, trousers, shirts and Jeans for the leading fashion labels across the world.

4.1.1.1 Major innovation strategies

a. New-to-the-world products: The Company has recently launched a first-of-its-kind, anti-viral technology-based fabric–VIRASAFE, which has been proven effective to fight against bacteria and viruses and also is an anti-odour fabric. It also pioneered the innovative concept of 'Customised Clothing' via launching of 'Raymond Made to Measure'.

b. New product lines: Since inception, Raymond has been heralded for creating numerous pioneering innovations in turn creating a leadership position for itself in the market and specifically catering to the mass and premium class of customers. The company has strong fibre-to-fabric manufacturing capabilities and is a textile powerhouse with state-of-the-art modern infrastructure and led by the strong product development team with collaborations with Italian designers. Raymond has on offer a wide range of quality shirting and suiting fabrics across a plethora of options such as Worsted Fabrics, Cotton, Wool blends, Linen, and Denim. It has also emerged as the largest over-the-counter (OTC) branded shirting player in the domestic organised market since its launch in 2015. The company recently launched 'All Black Collection' which has been the most comprehensive collection ever launched with over 1000 styles of black suiting fabric and it was like a poetic ode to the black fabric.

c. Repositioning: The company, in the last 5 years has set its target to attract young consumers especially millennials and the corporate travellers whose preference has shifted towards smart, casual and 'wrinkle-free' fabrics.

4.1.2 Siyaram's silks

Siyaram Silk Mills Ltd. (SSM) is part of the Siyaram Poddar Group, which is a small cap company with a market cap of Rs. 936.75 Cr. In 2013 the company was voted as the most trusted brand by Economic times and Nielsen Media Research. It is headquartered in the Kamala Mills compound, Lower Parel, Mumbai and has an integrated distribution network of over 0.1 million retail footprints and 170 branded showrooms spread across the country. It is India's largest producer of blended high fashion suiting/shirting fabrics in India and enjoys the unparalleled legacy of being the most preferred brand of both urban and rural India for four decades now as it has carved a niche in the wardrobe and hearts of its elite loyalists for creating a melange of cultural intricacies and avant-garde which has been synonymous with high quality, continuous innovation and iconic futuristic designs that are local at heart and international in appeal.

4.1.2.1 Major innovation strategies

a. New product lines: With a firm belief in business ethics and corporate sustainability and its cutting-edge in-house research and development team, Siyaram's ably houses an annual production of over 80 million meters of fabrics annually which provides a diverse range of fabrics such as polyester, viscose, polyester cotton, 100% cotton, 100% wool, 100% linen, TR, etc. Being an ISO 9001:2008 certified company, Siyaram's has garnered an expertise in every facet of production including weaving, dyeing, finishing, and garmenting. In 1991, the company ventured into the readymade garment segment by introducing Oxemberg, in 1995 launched J. Hampstead in the market with 100% pure worsted suiting fabrics in India and in 2001 it launched Mistair, a premium suiting brand meant particularly for high end class. In 2004, the brand launched its new product lines in the form of uniform, children's clothing, and a women's brand named 'Siya' and further plans to develop an exclusive range of fabrics in long staple cotton, Giza cotton, linen, wool cashmere, wool-silk-linen, silk, wool blends, and jacketing fabrics in linen. Later in 2015, the Company announced its global venture with a prominent Italian brand, Cadini.

4.1.3 Van Huesen

Van Heusen is India's premium fashion brand for men and women from Aditya Birla Fashion and Retail Limited and is all about modernity, sharpness, energy and heritage with its stylish, exclusive and trendy designs.

4.1.3.1 Major innovation strategies

a. New-to-the-world products: The brand is credited with the launching of several innovations in the market such as 'best white shirt in 2015'. Recently, the brand has launched another innovative solution that has revolutionised every consumer's wardrobe which is labelled as 'MYFIT' Collection whose USP lies in creating the perfect fitting garment across every body type, a brilliant feat achieved by any readymade apparel brand for the first time in the country. The brand is getting 100 orders every day under MYFIT Collection within 3 months of its launch. Yet another innovative range of formal wear Collection was launched by the Company in the form of 7-in-1 Suit Collection, which happened to be a unique concept. The collection allows flexibility for the wearer to get seven different looks from a distinct suit combination which comprises blazer, a reversible waistcoat and not one but two knitted trousers. With the launch of this bold and impactful range of occasion wear the brand has challenged the stereotype dressing (that a single classic suit can be donned not only once but multiple times during separate occasions, taking the fashion quotient to a new high). Featuring a repertoire of colours in warm earthy tones to colder shades of blue and stone, the collection highlights the dynamic transformation, efficiency and power.

The brand has always been developing new apparel technology to enhance the quality, comfort and style of its existing ranges. Some of its popular product lines are: (i) Van Heusen Commuter: power to move with built in Flex technology representing versatility, comfort and style whether running between boardrooms or jet-setting the globe; (ii) Van Heusen Performa: suits crafted with cutting edge Nano-Technologies and high-twist yarn to help one handle the tough times of life; (iii) Van Heusen Move: this collection was introduced with Future Fit Stretch Technology for unrivalled flexibility and freedom of movement in business wear by blending 98% wool with 2% elastane for enhanced flexibility and (iv) Van Heusen Evercool: this collection combines two revolutionary technologies to bring to the customers one of the 'coolest suit' in the market which was developed in Switzerland through Scholler technologies and cold-black technology that enables dark fabrics to reflect UV and Infrared heat and light.

b. New product lines: Seizing the opportunity of 'Work from Home' due to Covid-19, Van Heusen has recently launched its 'sub-brand Denim Labs' with a new campaign featuring actor Jacqueline Fernandes in the 'new blue'. Van Heusen's product design and R&D team is constantly churning new ideas for expansion which has launched its range of Innerwear, Athleisure, Active wear, lab-licenced masks (with germicidal technology that claims to disable the Sars-Cov2 virus on contact).

c. Repositioning: With these new lines of production, the company attempts to target consumers in the age group of 20–35 who majorly happen to be youngsters entering the job market as mid-level and senior-level professionals.

4.2 Casual/sportswear/active-wear

Some of the well-known brands under the category of Casual/Active/Sportswear in the Indian market are Mufti, Indian Terrain, Flying Machine, Provogue and Allen Solly (**Table 2**). Their NPD strategies are discussed below.

4.2.1 Mufti

4.2.1.1 Opportunity identification

The 90s was a period where India was going through a transition in fashion and the creators of this brand, Mr. Kamal Kushlani saw an opportunity to create a casualwear

Strategy of product innovation	Mufti	Flying machine	Allen Solly
New-to-the-world products	✓	✓	
New product lines	✓	✓	✓
Additions to the product Lines/product improvement		✓	
Repositioning			
Cost reductions			✓

Source: Author's own assessment of the Product Portfolio of the Apparel brands.

Table 2.
Strategies of new product development in the casual/active-wear clothing segment.

brand which became the first global fashion brand with Indian roots. Mufti was launched in 1998 with one driving ambition, to provide an alternative dressing solution, that did not conform to the 'uniform' codes of mainstream fashion. It currently retails through more than 1500 points of sale across India and has its own website to offer products via online shopping all over India. It has also implemented below-the-line approach in terms of niche marketing and distributed flyers at high-traffic routes, motels and malls. The company has been continuously putting out new designs without any substantial repetition which has gained it a huge recognition among the casual-wear oriented youth consumers and it soon became the most edgy casualwear brand even picked up by the celebrity stylists. The designs have been inspired through a rich interaction of culture, travel, people and places which are quite imaginative and convey Indian spirit with International codes of fashion.

4.2.1.2 Major innovation strategies

a. New-to-the-world products: It introduced club wear, street wear joggers from denim and turn-up sleeves which were hitherto unknown in the Indian market and was the first to make an entire range of jeans in stretch (for men), that was later adopted by the world. The brand revolutionised the basic category of shirts, which were of free-size and silhouette in the late 90s by shortening their length and making them tapered at the waist. After a couple of years they started selling jeans with Lycra and went against the conventional rough and tough denim fabric to suit the needs of the travelling and active consumer.

b. New product lines: When athleisure fashion spread in the market like wildfire with sudden influx of joggers, Mufti started creating denim joggers to provide durability to this popular product category.

4.2.2 Flying machine

Flying Machine is India's first home-grown denim brand owned by Arvind Mills' garments division and one of the coolest youth apparel brands in the country. The company was launched in the year 1980 when only smuggled jeans was available in the market. By 1994 it had become a leader in branded jeans in India and is still seen as a trendy and premium casualwear brand. The brand chooses to be a trendsetter rather than a fad-follower and this attitude is reflected in each and every of its products. Flying Machine is primarily a B and C town brand and has been synonymous with authentic details, original graphics, first in class urban innovation and true Italian styling.

4.2.2.1 Major innovative strategies

a. New-to-the-world products: Flying machine has attained 23 times rise in its Gross Merchandise Value (GMV) by deploying Rubicon technology which has not only increased its online visibility, but also strengthened its marketplace business and sales quite significantly.

b. New product lines: The Company follows the fashion cycle and plans only 60–70% of their collection in advance and do the rest 30% on the run. It recently launched the 'Young and Bold' Collection targeting the college students and early first jobbers between the age group 15–21. They have recently launched women's wear and party wear and related accessories which is also receiving a good response from the customers. In 2007, as a part of its re-launch phase, the brand roped in Italian designer Chicco (pronounced Khee-co) to help reinvent its design philosophy to be able to cater to an all-new Indian consumer. While Chicco was brought on board to take design to the next level, JHP-London was signed on to partner the brand's transformation at the retail level. As a result, the brand achieved a remarkable makeover through a new and urban store-format across the country.

c. Additions to the product lines: Flying Machine's five-pocket jeans with elaborate washes, for graphics, cut and sew details are the most popular under this category.

4.2.3 Allen Solly

The Aditya Birla apparel brand 'Allen Solly' is one of the exclusive brands that entered in the Indian market in 1993. Founded by William Hollin in 1744, Allen Solly is an extensive brand focussing on western style dressing and has set the trend in the changing workplace culture by introducing casual work apparels for working men and women. This product concept became very successful in the Indian market as work culture in India became much more relaxed than before, with the advent of the multinational companies into the Indian market which started relaxing their formal dressing norms worldwide. The company works extensively work over new designs with changes in fashion trends and with the extensive dynamic market in the textile industry, the brand has maintained its brand image with maintained quality and customer services. The brand can be best seen as 'comfort wear' for the young working professionals (in the age-group of 24–28 years) primarily based in Metro and Tier-I cities.

4.2.3.1 Major innovation strategies

a. New product lines: Recently the brand has launched the 'Go' trousers – a combination of stretch and wrinkle-free work trousers. The brand has also added new categories to its product line – tee shirts, winter-wear, suits, blazers and basic accessories such as ties, belts and socks. Recently the brand has introduced the concept of 'Friday Dressing' for women also which represents more of a relaxed work wear rather than strictly being formal. Ideas of 'Friday dressing' was specially introduced to target working people and their need of looking cool on Fridays in the office. Infact this is the only brand so far in the Indian market which is specifically focussed on women's professional as well as comfort dressing.

b. Cost reduction strategies: The strong supply chain network of the Aditya Birla Group has largely helped the brand to minimise its costs and deliver its products at an affordable price range as the brand targets young customers majorly.

4.3 Traditional/ethnic wear

Among the traditional clothing segments the most popular brands in the Indian market are Biba, Manyavar and Fabindia (**Table 3**).

4.3.1 Biba

Biba was first launched by Meena Bindra in 1988 with a small boutique in Mumbai. Today, it is a market leader in affordable occasion wear and with a legacy of over two decades, has been the emissary of evolving fashion for the modern Indian women of substance and strength by presenting them with beautiful and elegant ethnic wear which are much more than just traditional silhouettes. Biba became the first national brand to be recognised for its ethnic wear and ethnic-western mix and is currently available in 230 physical stores across 105 Indian cities and is also planning to take it to the overseas market as well. The label has been growing at a CAGR of more than 30% for the last 5 years and has also partnered with major retail chains such as Lifestyle and Central.

The brand has recently launched a new logo which has been inspired from a 'peacock feather', representing elegance and pride. The font has also been changed while the red colour has been retained from the old logo as it sits very well with the fashion codes and has a very rich association with Indian beauty and glamour. Anjan Roy, Director, Elephant Delhi, the branding firm that has worked closely with the key stakeholders at Biba to develop the new identity informed that, 'the typography of the new logo has been made more classic, so that it endures the test of time and still stands out as a young, vibrant and fashionable identity'.

4.3.1.1 Major innovation strategies

a. New product lines: The brand has recently introduced a children's wear range and also sells textiles. It also launched its first-ever brand campaign conceptualised by Lowe Lintas Bangalore. BIBA believes that there is a lot more to a woman than just her beauty, and that's what inspired the brand's Spring Summer 2017 Collection – "Who's that Girl". In the due course of time it has also launched Sleepwear and Loungewear Collection which are targeted for the mid-level

Strategy of product innovation	Biba	Manyavar	Fabindia
New-to-the-world products			
New product lines	✓	✓	✓
Additions to the product lines/product improvement			
Repositioning	✓		
Cost reductions			✓

Source: Author's own assessment of the Product Portfolio of the Apparel brands.

Table 3.
Strategies of new product development in the traditional/ethnic wear clothing segment.

segment of women who look for style, comfort and quality. The sleepwear category is emerging as a trending fashion, with bridal sleepwear and sleepwear for themed parties gaining increased traction, which acts as a key driver of the market. It recently forged a joint venture with designer Manish Arora, picking up a 51% stake and the new contemporary Indian wear collection would be known as 'Indian by Manish Arora'. The company also plans to expand its premium collection 'BIBA by Rohit Bal'.

b. Repositioning: After completing nearly 20 years, the brand is now segmenting the market by entering the luxury and bridal segments. It plans to further segment the estimated Rs 90,000-crore ethnic market by entering the mass market with either a new brand or through an acquisition. Gradually it launched a value-fashion brand *Rangriti*, which offers daily/casual wear in the range of Rs. 500–Rs. 2000, to appeal to the masses, which has generated Rs. 60 crore of the sales already.

4.3.2 Manyavar

Known for offering exclusive ethnic-inspired clothing at affordable prices, the brand caters to confident, charming and stylish men who proudly flaunt their 'desi avatar' on weddings, parties and other special occasions. There was a huge void in the men's ethnic wear segment in India and it was over-looked by all the big existing players in the market. No brand considered ethnic wear as 'fashion' or even a category to start with. It is in this period that Manyavar was launched by Ravi Modi in 1999 by bringing in some of the country's finest fashion designers and artisans under one roof. The philosophy of the brand is to transcend cultural and ethnic sensibilities to establish Indian wear as a widely accepted and preferred clothing not only in India but at the global level. The brand has also won several awards and accolades for its pioneering efforts in revitalising ethnic fashion and achieving several milestones in retail business. Today, Manyavar sells its gorgeous *sherwanis* and *kurtas* through more than 400 outlets located across 200 cities worldwide. The brand garnered INR 820 crore in revenue during FY19 and has been growing at CAGR of 20 percent in the last 5 years.

Each of its products is a signature product; it is a manifestation of in-depth research, creativity and design, workmanship, technology and benchmarking. Off-beat colours like pastels, which were never seen in a groom's palette, have acquired a large space in men's ethnic wear range. The brand also incorporated in its design asymmetrical cuts and hemlines which have been recently trending and making the whole range of men's wear all the more exciting and innovative. It should be noted that Manyavar is one of those rare brands that started advertising through theatres, first in the year 2014. Its early video campaigns were made exclusively for theatre consumption – pre-movie campaigns and interval spots.

4.3.2.1 Major innovation strategies

a. New product lines: Manyavar started with wedding wear and has over time forayed into celebration, festive and casual wear and later on developed fusion wear. The modern-day brand not only targeted the man of the house but expanded its focus on the whole family, introducing newer collections and also sought to popularise Indian wear for everyday use through lines of cotton *kurtas* and *pyjamas*. In the same year, in a breakthrough development, Manyavar launched its women's ethnic wear collection – 'Mohey' which was created to sell particularly traditional wear like lehengas and saris for women. Not leaving behind juniors, the brand also started with Kid's Ethnic and Fusion Wear line and launched premium men's wear brand – *Twamev* last year. Apart from this, the timeless celebration collection of the brand includes exquisite Sherwanis, Indo-Westerns, Royal Bandhgalas, Classic Kurta-Jackets, and fashion kurtas.

4.3.3 Fabindia

4.3.3.1 Opportunity identification

During the British rule, the handloom industry of India was badly affected due to the advent of power-looms and heavy taxes. Post-independence, the Khadi movement launched by the Father of the Nation, M. K. Gandhi did revive the handloom and textile industry to a certain extent however, with the deepening industrialisation and power looms, cheap and convenient cloth became the norm of the working class. This even caused the weaver population to diminish significantly while forcing them to change their professions as agricultural labourers, daily wage earners making them more and more desperate and vulnerable.

This was the time when Fab India was founded by John Bissell in 1960 who saw a tremendous potential in the handloom textiles of India. The Company started as an Export business at John's home in New Delhi, exporting furnished goods and subsequently hand-woven fabric to the overseas customers. In 1998, John Bissell passed away, letting his son William Bissell take over the reins. Today Fabindia has become the largest retailer for handloom and handcrafted products in India with more than 300 stores worldwide, an interwoven network of more than 50,000 weavers and 90,000 artisans scattered all over India.

The brand has a unique marketing strategy of connecting with customers through meaningful stories rather than spending big budget on advertising. It organises crafts mornings where artisans speak about their art and experts are invited to speak on importance of using organic products and environmental production. Fabindia has been a brand which is a blend of urban contemporary designs with traditional craftsman techniques, which attracted the urban populace and gave popularity to Fabindia over government owned emporiums. The company has been involved in various CSR activities and is one of the most known brand in India for its work towards the society and has won many awards and accolades for it.

4.3.3.2 Major innovation strategies

a. New product lines: Its portfolio is broadly categorised into traditional women's, men's and kids' clothing and accessories. The brand also offers western dresses under Fabel brand.

b. Cost reduction strategies: The target customer of company is middle class consumers in cities of India and abroad and that is why it has adopted competitive pricing for most of its products. However, Fab India applies product line pricing for each of its product wherein a base price is set for the high price sensitive consumer segment and higher quality products are marketed to less price sensitive consumer segment at a premium over the base price. It also does promotional pricing by offering its product at discount prices for a window of time.

4.4 All categories apparel brands

The major brands under this category are Westside, Pantaloons and Zara (**Table 4**).

4.4.1 Westside

In the late 1990s, the popular Indian female attire the salwar kameez completely changed its look. The dupatta was set aside, 'the bottom' evolved to what is now known as the leggings, palazzos and pants, while the top metamorphosed into the era-defining garment, the 'kurti' which completely changed the Indian female ready-made garment sector. Leading this fashion revolution – from a store in south Mumbai's Hughes Road precinct – was Tata group's flagship retail store Westside. Westside was established by Mrs. Simone Tata when she acquired the Littlewoods in 1998. Twenty years on, the retail store is now a chain of large-format department stores with 28 in-house brands and 132 stores across the country and constitutes about 96% of Trent revenue, the retail arm of the Tata group.

While an exclusive range of own branded fashion apparel continues to be the mainstay of the chain, the Westside model involves active control all across the value chain including branding, sourcing, logistics, distribution, pricing, display and promotion of almost 90% of the product range retailed. Priced moderately, Westside, over the years, has garnered its own set of loyalists, who prefer the blend of cutting-edge fashion with a touch of Indian-ness. The styles that make it into the shopping basket go through a rigorous process of approvals, starting with the blue seal, silver seal and the final gold seal – each seal, a level of approval for pattern, design, colour palette, etc. The 'value for money' tag still sticks, but the styles have gotten bolder, cuts edgier and colours funkier.

4.4.1.1 Major innovation strategies

a. New product lines: Recently Westside has launched trending-across-the-globe 'mini-me' range for children: chino trousers and polo necks for kids who want to imitate their dad's Friday-dressing or Utsa dresses for little girls.

   Some of the key brands in women's wear segment are (i) Bombay Paisley: chic, western and contemporary ethnic wear for the experimental and vibrant youth, (ii) Gia: a fashionable casual collection for the curvy women, (iii) L.O.V: is a

Strategy of product innovation	Westside	Pantaloons	Zara
New-to-the-world products			
New product lines	✓	✓	✓
Additions to the product lines/product improvement	✓		✓
Repositioning			
Cost reductions			

Source: Author's own assessment of the Product Portfolio of the Apparel brands.

Table 4.
Strategies of new product development in all categories apparel brands.

smart, casual, feminine offering for the 25-plus women and (iv) Zuba: silk and handloom blends with handcrafted embroidery. Other noteworthy brands include Wardrobe, a trendy 9-to-9 fashion for women and Nuon, a young casual fashion brand. In the men's category, Westside has Ascot, a modern classic lifestyle brand for the discerning man, E.T.A, understated casual wear for contemporary men, and West Sport offers functional and stylish casual mens apparel. In FY'15, the chain launched four new brands, exclusively available at Westside stores. It brought in Wunder Love, the chain's in-house lingerie brand and Sassy Soda, Westside's collection of trendy clothing designed for the curvier youth. Apart from tying up with renowned designers such as Narendra Kumar, Priyadarshini Rao, Krishna Mehta, Westside has also tied up exclusively with international brands such as Italian kids wear brand Chicco, Woolworths Bath and Body.

b. Additions to the product lines/product improvement: Westside took fast fashion a step further by being the first Indian company to launch the *Fast N Fab concept.* A capsule collection of three to four looks in each brand hits select stores on the third Friday of each month. Sophisticated fashion forecasting models; designers travelling to fashion capitals across the globe to imbibe ideas and styles; teams sourcing raw material from the remotest parts of India; buyers meeting artisans and vendors across the country has made it possible for Westside to remain fast and fashionable.

4.4.2 Pantaloons

Pantaloons, a division of Aditya Birla Fashion and Retail Limited (ABFRL) Group, has been one of the strongest and most preferred brand in the Indian fashion retail industry among the large retail format stores over the past two decades. Over the period of time, it has evolved into a progressive style partner for the fashion seeking shopper by positioning itself as a spontaneous, playful, vibrant brand which is at the forefront of all fashion trends across all categories. It has built one of India's widest retail network with more than 340 large format stores. This year, Pantaloons focused on growing Pantaloons.com, its online store which recorded 2.3 times of sales over the last year. Pantaloons reported an annual revenue of Rs. 1859 crore, down by 47% from last year, while the EBITDA[1] margin stands at Rs. 276 crore compared to Rs. 563 crore last year and was positive (14.8%) for FY21.

With good design capabilities, innovative product development, agile supply chain and customer-centric processes, Pantaloons delivers an enhanced Omni-channel shopping experience to its customers. Today, the Company is at the cusp of a strategic shift of its missions from process-centric to product-centric approach[2] from 2020 to 2025, where products will be at the fulcrum of the Company's sustainability strategy. The Company has also built on its Digital Trade Show platform, replacing seasonal tradeshows, which have been the mainstay of the industry. This has helped completely transform the product development lifecycle, right from the design stage. While the Company celebrates a leadership position in the fashion segment and continues to

[1] EBTDA stands for earnings before interest, taxes, depreciation and amortisation. The EBITDA margin is a measure of a company's operating profit as a percentage of its revenue.

[2] The product-centric approach for any company attempts to identify key focus areas for improvement and develop interventions for each life cycle stage of the product, including upstream and downstream operations.

grow brand equity and consumer base, the Company is always working towards giving back to the environment through 'ReEarth' sustainability philosophy and has won several accolades for it at the international level.

4.4.2.1 Major innovation strategies

a. New product lines: In line with its strategy to increase its private label share, Pantaloons launched new categories including Home, Sarees, Bags and other Accessories and has also unveiled exclusive brands in women's ethnic wear. The year 2020 was the turning point in its ethnic strategy when the company acquired Jaypore brand while in 2021, with two fresh partnerships with Tarun Tahiliani and Sabyasachi, the company now boasts of the most comprehensive portfolio of iconic ethnic wear brands across price points in the domestic markets. Furthermore, the Company announced new strategic investments in luxury couture Sabyasachi, and men's ethnic and ceremonial wear by Tarun Tahiliani. Some of its brands include: Ajile, Bare Denim, Indus Route, People, Richard Parker, Rig, SF Jeans and Urban Ranger.

4.4.3 Zara

Zara is the well-known face of one the world's most innovative retail groups Inditex (world's largest fashion and clothing companies). Zara is a Spanish clothing and accessories retailer based in Arteixo, Galicia, Spain and founded in 1975 by Armancio Ortega. The philosophy of the company is to get new fashions fastest to the market as it just takes less than 4 weeks for the company to take its designs to the store shelves. During the 1980s, Zara started changing the design, manufacturing, and distribution process to reduce lead times. This allowed them to react to new trends in a quicker way, in what they called "instant fashions." Zara has been famously described by Louis Vutton designer, Daniel Piette as "Possibly the most innovative and devastating retailer in the world".

The company has already gone global while selling on all the five continents and generating great economies of scale. There are over 2000 Zara stores located across 88 countries. The process of innovation at Zara does not apply only to products but also towards streamlining and optimising manufacturing, supply chain management, data tracking, inventory management, store layout and staff operations. From its humble origins in 1975 in Galicia, Spain, Zara developed a successful strategy that has led it to rapidly design, produce and distribute fashionable clothing to the customers worldwide. Gradually it also developed in-house capabilities in design, low-cost production, supply chain optimisation and effective feedback loops to ensure that it continually delivers great products to its customers.

The Zara design team consists of 350 people who are completely anonymous and are charged with generating and delivering 18,000 new product designs in a year. At Zara's headquarters in Arteixo La Coruna, Spain, there are 25 full-size shop windows with differing displays and lighting which enables the designers to look through the format of the retail stores and design accordingly. Zara also has a flat hierarchal management structure with designers empowered to make fast decisions. Only 15%–25% of clothes are produced before the season and 50%–60% at the start of the season. All of these competitive advantages have led Zara to an enviable position where it does not need to advertise. Its core values are found in four simple terms: beauty, clarity, functionality and sustainability.

5. Conclusions

5.1 Key policy perspectives for the future

The present study attempted to examine various strategies and methods towards New Product Development adopted by some of the prominent global players operating in the Indian Textile market. Some of the important observations are summarised below.

Firstly, if we analyse the segmentation of the Indian clothing market, we find that it is majorly flooded with men's apparel segment while almost completely neglecting the women side which may seem to be a huge gap to be addressed and infact probably somewhat been seen as an opportunity by the multinational brands who have exploited it in the later part of the 20th century. Infact the formal clothing segment as represented by two major Indian players: The Raymond Group and Siyaram's particularly cater to the men's clothing range only. With the advent of the multinational brands like Allen Solly into the Indian markets, we could find women's formal as well as comfort casual clothing range has been given due attention over the period of time. It may also seem that women's apparel garments only came into being after the substantial rise in their numbers in the workplace otherwise their might be a connotation in the minds of the companies that formal wear is only about men's clothing and perhaps the monopoly of it.

Secondly, the casual/comfort wear clothing is the largest category in terms of market size and a lot of small and large players have come up which though not mentioned in the current paper but constitute a substantial market size in the Indian Readymade Garments Industry. Thus there is a lot of scope in New Product Development in this category of clothing segment which so far has not been done by the Indian brands which have largely followed the trends and patterns of international brands.

Thirdly, the discussions in the above sections have confirmed the hypothesis that the most sought after strategies of New Product Development has been launching of the New Product Lines followed by the Additions to the Product Lines/Product Improvement. New-to-the-World Products has been particularly pursued by the multinational brands like Van Heusen. Apart from this, it is also to be realised by the apparel brands that apart from the elite section, India has a large middle income segment which can be cashed on to the fullest potential. But so far the brands only have capitalised on the premium and elite class.

Thus there is a need for the Indian brands to catch up with the multinational brands so as to become more competitive in the domestic and overseas markets which would only be possible by developing an extensive innovation culture and capabilities of the small innovative firms on the part of the policy making institutions in India.

Author details

Mitali Gupta
Independent Researcher and Consultant, New Delhi

*Address all correspondence to: miafgr2809@gmail.com

References

[1] Cooper RG. Winning at New Products. 3rd ed. New York: Addison Wesley; 2001. pp. 130-141

[2] Drucker P. Entrepreneurship and Innovation: Practice and Principles. New York: Harper Business; 1985

[3] OECD. Innovation to Strengthen Growth and Address Global and Social Challenges. Paris: OECD Publishing; 2005

[4] The Global Innovation Index (GII). Effective Innovation Policies for Development [Internet]. 2015. Available from: https://www.globalinnovationindex.org/userfiles/file/reportpdf/GII-2015-v5.pdf

[5] Kiraka R, Kobia, Katwalo K. Micro, Small and Medium Enterprise Growth and Innovation in Kenya: A Case Study on the Women Enterprise Fund. Investment Climate and Business Environment Research Fund Report. 2013

[6] Hamid A, Tasmin R. The relationship of business innovation capabilities and technology innovation capabilities on SME organisations: A conceptual framework. In: Proceedings of the 2nd International Conference on Global Optimization and its Application, Malaysia. 2013

[7] Mohd Rosli M, Sidek S. The impact of innovation on the performance of small and medium manufacturing enterprises: Evidence from Malaysia. Journal of Innovation Management in Small and Medium Enterprises. 2013;**2013**:16. Article ID: 885666. DOI: 10.5171/2013.885666

[8] Acs JZ, Autio E, Szerb L. National systems of entrepreneurship: Measurement issues and policy implications. Research Policy. 2014;**43**(3):476-494

[9] Akis E. Innovation and competitive power. In: World Conference on Technology, Innovation and Entrepreneurship, Procedia—Social and Behavioral Sciences. Vol. 195. 2015. pp. 1311-1320

[10] European Commission. Green Paper on Innovation [Internet]. 1995. Available from: http://europa.eu/documents/comm/green_papers/pdf/com95_688_en.pdf

[11] Ramadani V, Gërguri S. Innovation: Principles and strategies. Strategic Change. 2011;**20**(3-4):101-110

[12] European Innovation Management Academy. 2016. Available from: https://www.improveinnovation.eu

[13] Schumpeter J. Business Cycles: A Theoretical, Historical and Statistical Analysis of the Capitalist Process. Vol. 2. New York: Mc Graw-Hill; 1939

[14] Booz A, Hamilton. New Products Management for the 1980s. New York, NY: Author; 1982

[15] Crawford M, Benedetto AD. New Products Management. 7th ed. New York: McGraw-Hill; 2003

[16] Kumar S, Phrommathed P. New Product Development: An Empirical Study of the Effects of Innovation Strategy, Organisation Learning and Market Conditions. New York: Springer; 2005. pp. 55-57